Eco-Villages

&

Sustainable Communities

© Gaia Trust & Findhorn Foundation, 1995
First published 1996
Reprinted 1996, 1997

ISBN 1 899171 21 5

British Library Cataloguing-in-Publication Data.
A catalogue record for this book is available from the British Library.

Edited by Jillian Conrad, with the help of Drew Withington.
Set in Palatino by Findhorn Press.

"Wild Geese" from *Dream Work* by Mary Oliver. © Mary Oliver 1985.
Used by permission of Grove/Atlantic, Inc.

Photographs © Findhorn Foundation Visual Arts.
Cover design by Posthouse Printing & Publishing.
Printed and bound by J. W. Arrowsmith Ltd., Bristol, England.

♻ Printed on recycled paper.

Published by
Findhorn Press
The Park, Findhorn
Forres IV36 0TZ
Scotland
tel +44 (0)1309 690582
fax +44 (0)1309 690036
e-mail thierry@findhorn.org
http://www.mcn.org/findhorn/press
or http://www.gaia.org/findhornpress/

Eco-Villages

Sustainable Communities

Models for 21st Century Living

FINDHORN
Press

Contents

workshops

resources

FOREWORD

The week-long conference on "Eco-Villages and Sustainable Communities: Models for the 21st Century", held at the Findhorn Foundation in October, 1995, was an extraordinary gathering. For one week, over 400 people were asked to share not only their knowledge and ideas, but their passions and personalities. The conference brought together different aspects of what it means to live collaboratively, as well as privately, encompassing the built environment, the natural world, and our inner lives. Yet it wasn't the size and breadth of the conference that were most remarkable, but the level of engagement that infused every plenary, workshop and conversation that was shared. It was the kind of participation that comes from genuine enthusiasm and curiosity, from glimpsing life as a wonderful multitude of possibilities.

Broadly stated, eco-villages and sustainable communities are holistic models for dwelling that respect the many variables that make people and places vibrant, particular and lasting. How these variables are woven together is different for each individual and group. And that is precisely the point. Perhaps a good way to think of what we have come to call 'eco-villages' and 'sustainability' are as a collection of possibilities — environmental, economical, social, technological and spiritual — and our task is to create a pattern or design, weaving them together to the best of our abilities.

This will take patient effort. How do we sustain something — be it our local economy or the planets' natural systems — in the face of rapid change and evolution? It can seem contradictory to speak of local economies and global villages in the same breath. How do these two extremes, the local and the global, come together? Or, are they separate at all? These seeming contradictions come together in the act of participation. Only by actively engaging in the possibilities presented by these questions, testing them out in particular, physical places, can eco-villages and sustainable communities become widespread patterns for living and dwelling.

The task is not to confirm what is, but to prepare for what could be. These Proceedings are meant to encourage this kind of participation. They are a tool for furthering the exchange of ideas and enthusiasm that took place at the conference. They highlight some of the most enticing possibilities that can be a part of the future. But it has been difficult to adequately express the incredible feeling of good will that coursed through the week of the conference. The plenaries and workshops that appear here have been shortened and lack the visual images that helped to illustrate them. Still, the essence of the conference remains. The gathering at Findhorn was something more than a conference, it was a unique meeting of mind and spirit. Hopefully, by communicating the essence of that meeting, the lively participation and enthusiasm that it set in motion can continue.

Jillian Conrad
Editor

ECO-VILLAGES AND SUSTAINABLE COMMUNITIES: MODELS FOR SUSTAINABLE LIVING IN THE 21ST CENTURY

"Eco-Villages are human scale, full-featured communities, both urban and rural, that are integrated harmlessly into the natural environment and can successfully continue into the indefinite future..."
Robert Gilman, excerpted from the *Eco-Village Report*.

Dear Friends,

Co-creating and coordinating this conference with my good friend John Talbott, has been the highlight of my life so far. It enabled me to bring together many years of learning, experimenting, networking and relationship building. I see sustainability as the context out of which human life can continue on the planet, and this conference was an important step in that direction.

I have watched the awareness of sustainability grow over the years. When my husband, Robert, and I founded Context Institute sixteen years ago, sustainability was one of those words we had to explain every time we used it. Today, it is embraced globally, by communities in the underdeveloped nations as well as the developed nations, by both urban and rural groups. People are understanding that the present way of living cannot be sustained in the long term, and for many the quality of life is already deteriorating. We are looking for better ways of living; and ecovillages are providing useful models and guidelines for sustainable living.

New solutions are available to help us live in ways that simultaneously meet human needs, protect the environment, and enhance our quality of life. They range from better developed means of communication, conflict resolution and decision making, to appropriate technologies, from building, to waste treatment. The transformation of fundamental human attitudes underlying our destructive impact on nature requires a deeper look at their causes. In order to solve the environmental crisis we must also look at the social and cultural crisis; we must also look at sustainable economics as much as ecological technologies. I am very excited about the growing awareness and creative solutions that support a future based on the cycles of nature, the foundation of life.

The conference was a gathering of people who have been at the forefront of making the needed changes in their own communities and lives. Their idealism and practical experience is an inspiration. They — we — have built a strong body of practical skills with both an urban focus, such as the Eco-City movement, and with a rural focus, through, for example, the Global Eco-village Network.

The biggest challenges that I see to a sustainable future are despair, hopelessness, closed mindedness and greed. These are all human traits that block us from living happy lives in harmony with ourselves, each other and nature. Moving to a sustainable future is not a technical problem. The technologies are available. It's a human problem.

Can we become educated, inspired and open hearted enough to move quickly and embrace the problems the world faces; or will we continue with business as usual in the hope that "someone else" will solve the big problems? Well folks, we are the "someones" who have created the big problems — and we are the "someones" who through each of our contributions, will make a step towards the solutions. It's up to all of us.

Best wishes for a sustainable and positive future!

Diane A. Gilman
Conference Co-Coordinator

P.S. A Planted Seed and How It Grew

In August of 1993, John Talbott, Robert and I sat on a bench under several beautiful large trees at the International Intentional Communities Conference in Olympia, Washington, wondering how we could collaborate on something at Findhorn. This conversation is the seed from which the conference grew. Now we hope that its inspiration will spread far and wide for many years into the future. The whole experience felt blessed and guided along the way as decisions were made, ideas created, and problems solved — and all with a profoundly caring and nurturing staff. With their help and the enthusiasm of the participants, the conference has surpassed even our wildest dreams.

Dear Friends,

It is clear from all our global environmental indicators that the current pattern of destructive human activity or 'development' cannot continue, with little or no thought being given to the impact on the natural world that sustains us. What we need however, is not more bad news — but something that shows us a positive way forward. We need a vision of how humanity can work and live together in harmony with each other and the planet; a vision that will bring a sense of hope and inspiration to our path into the next century.

Our conference on Eco-Villages and Sustainable Communities, held here at Findhorn in October 1995, was such an experience. It was particularly poignant for those of us living in and around the Findhorn Foundation Community, as we have seen our own development here evolving into the eco-village model.

The definition of an eco-village as we have come to understand it represents a full featured 'human ecology' that is sustainable: spiritually, culturally, and economically, as well as ecologically. At Findhorn, we are strong in the cultural (community life) and spiritual areas, but have work to do in the areas of economics and the built environment: creating financially viable and environmentally sustainable lifestyles that meet our basic needs for adequate (but not extravagant) material comfort.

The preparation for the Conference helped us to define these two areas as our main challenges. And we have been given a wonderful opportunity to work on the practical development of these concepts. Just before the conference we were able to buy an adjacent six acres of land for building. We are now fully engaged in designing a layout that will form a critical piece of the eco-village here: 30+ homes with space for businesses, playing and community. A chance to bring dreams into reality! A new kind of 'development.'

What is it about sustainable communities and this strange modern version of the village that seems to be so appealing? I think it is that somewhere in each of us is the knowledge that a better way of living on our earth exists, that enriches us personally yet does not deplete or diminish our natural world. Perhaps it is some archetype of The Garden or another image of a harmonious life, but each of has that intuitive knowledge that it is possible. Today, we are beginning to think circularly instead of linearly. 'Human ecology' takes us beyond just the physical world, into our deeper needs as human beings and the meaning of life.

The response we recieved to the conference was a tremendous affirmation of this. In the 20 years that the Foundation has been hosting international conferences we have never had the kind of interest and enthusiasm that this event generated. In the end, we had nearly 400 people from 40 countries and many hundreds were turned away due to our limited space!

The conference week itself brought together many different aspects of sustainability. We tried to 'walk our talk' during the week and offer a diverse and varied experience of listening, seeing visual images of people's work, giving and taking workshops and doing hands on projects, like tree planting, and constructing a straw bale house and building a ceremonial earth lodge. The arts were incorporated at every possible moment with early morning singing, circle dancing, creative art workshops, performances in the plenary meetings and late night jam sessions. We also included a trade exhibition of environmental products and an outstanding book fair.

It was a great experience to work on the conference and to share that with Diane Gilman, my Co-Coordinator, and the dozens of people here who also helped. As a communtiy, we received a great boost that has helped us to move ahead with renewed inspiration and enthusiasm, urged on by those who came and witnessed what we have already done.

We hope that these proceedings will serve to encourage all of you who are also seeking solutions in your home towns and countries, as we move together towards the 21st Century.

John L. Talbott
Conference Co-Coordinator

THE GREAT AWAKENING   Peter Russell

What I want to do tonight is to move from the totally, utterly cosmic to the most deeply personal. Starting with the utterly cosmic.

The Universe is big; very, very, big. For every star you see with the naked eye there are billions, literally billions more in our galaxy that you never see, and for every star in our galaxy there is a galaxy in the Universe. We are literally just a speck in infinity. The same is true of time. If you chart the history of life on this planet up the side of the World Trade Centre, human beings appear about a fraction of an inch from the top, and our own lifetimes take up less than a thousandth of an inch. Our life experience is less than the thickness of a layer of paint on top. Indian teachings say that "Humanity is a blink in the eye of God." And that's just about right. If you take the amount of time it takes to blink an eye in your own lifetime, that's the amount of time we've been around. But what I want to show you tonight is that, insignificant as we may be in terms of space and time, I think we are in the middle of something very significant indeed here on Planet Earth.

Human beings are a species that has begun to explore and understand the world in which we live. Science now talks about reaching out in terms of three depths: deep space, looking out to the edges of the Universe; deep time, looking back to the beginning of the Universe; and deep structure, looking down into the depths of creation, the subatomic levels.

The knowledge we're gaining from this exploration we're turning into technology. Many of the things we've done with our information and communication technologies would have seemed like science fiction only 10-20 years ago. To be able to stick a piece of paper in a machine, and have it instantly reappear in Japan, was science fiction a few years ago. Now we can't look into the future more than five or ten years ahead, because the world is changing so fast.

The other side of the story is the unwelcome side effects that all of this change has brought. We've dealt with a lot of sickness and sanitation problems, and as a result our population has exploded. It's now 5.8 billion, and growing. Of these people 70% live in poverty. There is pollution, environmental degradation, and loss of biodiversity. And possibly the most worrying problem of all is the destruction of the ozone layer. The only reason life exists on land is because the ozone layer is there to protect us from ultra-violet light.

I don't think there's ever been a time in the history of humanity, or perhaps even in the history of the planet, when so much has been possible, but also so much has been at stake. And the obvious question is why it is that a species that can be so creative, and calls itself so intelligent, can also be so stupid? To realise we are destroying our environment, on which our own survival depends, and then to continue destroying it, is insane. Where did we go wrong?

Let's go back and look at how we got to this state. I want to look at evolution, not as biological evolution, but as the evolution of consciousness. **I believe all creatures are conscious. It isn't something purely human. I think that consciousness is as fundamental to the Universe as space, time and matter.** What has evolved along with the evolution of form and biology, is the contents of consciousness, what we are conscious of.

An analogy is to imagine a painting on a canvas. Every creature has the canvas, the faculty of consciousness. A simple cell has a very faint picture painted on that canvas. What has evolved as life is the quality of the picture; the dimensions, colour, and detail. As creatures evolved further they began to grow senses, and take in more information. To process that information they developed nervous systems. And from the evolution of fish onwards the main thrust of evolution has been on the inside; an explosion in the complexity and size of the nervous system. The end product has been brains such as man's; the most complex information processing systems in the known universe. Along with this growth in the nervous system has come a growth in consciousness.

After receiving degrees in theoretical physics, experimental psychology, and computer science, Peter Russell travelled to India to study meditation and Eastern philosophy. Since then, his focus has been the exploration and development of human consciousness, integrating Eastern and Western understandings of the mind. He has worked as a consultant to corporations such as IBM, and authored several books, including The Awakening Earth *and* The Global Brain Awakens.

What makes human beings special is almost an accident of evolution. It is that we can talk to each other. I say that it is an accident of evolution, because from what we now know chimpanzees and gorillas have the mental ability in their minds to speak. What they don't have is the voice box, and their tongue isn't as flexible. The accident that happened to humanity is that for some reason our voice box changed and our tongue freed up. We became able to communicate with each other, to share our experiences, and create collective knowledge. We're also able to use language internally, for thinking. Being able to communicate this interior world enabled us to develop communities based on the shared ideas, values and beliefs.

Out of this has come the realisation that we are conscious. And I think this is probably the greatest significance of all of human beings. The Universe has begun to wake up to itself through us. But at the moment we're only half awake. Self-consciousness is the fourth depth, what I call 'deep mind'. It's what the mystics have consistently said is the goal of all our explorations. It is as we explore this depth that we will begin to understand what spirituality has been about all these years.

In the last couple of years the whole subject of consciousness has moved back into science. I think this is going to be critically important for the whole sustainability movement. **If you look at the crisis that we are facing, it all comes back to human beings; to human greed, to love of money and love of power, and to the fact that we are not yet fully awake as to who we really are.** We all need to be self-centred enough to ensure that our basic needs are met for food, water, and shelter, and so on. If these needs are not met we feel bad, and if they are met, we feel at peace. Thus the fundamental motivation of every creature is to be at peace. What we're really looking for is nothing external, but a state of consciousness.

In our society, we have adopted the belief that if you are not at peace then there must be something wrong with the external world. Two hundred years ago life was very hard for most people, and this belief was probably valid. But the result of the Industrial Revolution has been that most people in the developed world don't lack for their basic needs. Yet our belief system decrees that if you have all of these things and are still not happy, then you must consume more, rather than looking within for the real, spiritual, answer.

So the crisis in the world is not just a crisis of environmental destruction, it is also a crisis of consciousness. Any crisis is a sign that the old way doesn't work anymore. In this case it is the old way of thinking, the old consciousness that is no longer working. As well as doing everything we can on the external level to be living in a more sustainable manner, it is an absolute imperative that we also look at the unsustainable consciousness that lies behind it. We need to begin to make a change of consciousness in ourselves.

I called this talk 'The Great Awakening', because there is something very significant happening now on this planet. There is a mass grassroots movement towards inner, spiritual awakening. We are beginning to wake up, and sharing it with each other, which accelerates the learning. In five years time we could be living in a totally different world in terms of consciousness.

This is where physical communities have a very, very important role to play, because we need the encouragement of others. One thing I've learned during my own spiritual journey is that I can't do it alone. We're here to remind each other and help each other. I think our relationships are our greatest spiritual teachers. I mention this because we're here at this conference to look at what we can do to really begin living in a more conscious, environmentally sound way, as communities. And I think the most important element of that means making a change in consciousness, within ourselves, and how we care for each other.

WHY ECO-VILLAGES?   Robert Gilman

Before looking at "Why eco-villages?" I want to start off by asking "What time is it?" I don't mean on our watches, but "Where are we in history?"

I want to look at where we are physically. This chart goes from 1900 to 2100. We're at the point where the two lines break apart. Up until now they've both been growing exponentially and they will continue to grow up to a point that systems theorists and ecologists like to describe as 'overshoot and collapse'. When any part of a system grows so big that it starts to destroy and erode the resources it depends on, then it overshoots its ability to be supported and it collapses. Biologists see this all the time. And there is no reason to suspect that we as a species are immune from it. That's the dotted line. But the good news for me in this diagram is the solid line. The solid line represent the way that the computer model shift, and the way that we could shift, making physically a very simple set of changes. I won't say simple socially, but simple physically. The changes are in three areas: technology, consumption and population.

I like to think of these three areas as a three legged stool. **When I hear arguments that say it is consumption or population or technology that we really need to work on, my response is 'Which leg of a three legged stool holds it up?'** I want to offer that as an image for us for this week.

To step into the issue of 'why communities?', if those are the changes that we need to make at a physical level, why is it that communities are important? There is absolutely no way for us to reasonably get to a sustainable society unless we address the

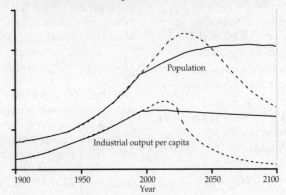

A Choice of Futures
Sustainable Development vs. Business As Usual

Policy and behavior changes that, if initiated in 1995, could lead to a sustainable future

Technology
• Decreased reliance on non-renewable resources per unit of industrial output (cut in half in 20 years through efficiency and renewables)
• Improved agricultural technologies and soil conservation
• Increased investment in pollution control (pollution production rate cut in half in 20 years)

Consumption
• Industrial output per capita limited to about 1995 levels. Standard of living grows through more useful products with longer lives

Population
• Complete availability of birth control methods
• Average desired family size of 2 children
• Increased investment in human services (by about 50%)

design of our communities. It is very critical that there be activities put in place as soon as possible to really change the degree to which our communities are committing us to huge levels of resource consumption. The good news is that in this room I know there are people who know how to take existing communities and enormously shrink energy use — and it's not just energy use — it's resource use and all kinds of other things. Technically we know what to do, but we're not yet doing it.

I think another very important dimension of asking 'what time is it?', is more the social and human side. Looking at issues of sustainable culture, I have found it has been very helpful to think in terms of three major epics in history and two important transitions between them. The first, the Tribal, has been our longest period of human experience. Then there was a transition to agriculture and cities, which led us to the age of Empire. I would suggest that we are now in the midst of a transition that is as profound. One of the things that makes our lives so seemingly schizophrenic is that we're living in an overlap of eras; a time when our day to day experience is much more characteristic of the era we're moving into, a Planetary era. Whereas our institutions all grow out of the past five thousand years of the Empire era. And when I say institutions I don't just mean governments, but also the mythologies we use and have inherited that are embedded in us.

One of the things that population growth and technology have done is to really shorten the feedback loops. The karma comes around and hits

After working as an astrophysicist for NASA twenty-five years ago, Robert Gilman decided that "the stars could wait, but the planet couldn't." Since then he has devoted himself to the study of global sustainability, futures research and strategies for positive social change. He and Diane Gilman are the co-founders of the Context Institute and In Context Journal.

Robert and Diane Gilman
Context Institute
P.O. Box 10396
Bainbridge Island
Washington 98110
USA

rgilman@context.org or
dgilman@context.org

Context Institute and
In Context:
http: //www.context.org

you in the face much sooner now. Not just on the basis of moral principle, but on the basis of what's really working. All kinds of groups are discovering that if I want to win, I better make sure that you win, and that the surrounding environment wins. We're being forced into, if you will, what has long been a moral position.

Where does this leave us relative to communities and eco-villages? I'd like to suggest that eco-villages and sustainable communities and eco-neighbourhoods, are ideally the places for working on bringing forth the new culture. You don't have culture until you have something you share with others. If we try to do it on a mega-scale, we're dealing with abstractions. The place where we can really discover each other and ourselves is the human scale.

When we wrote the Eco-Village Report for Gaia Trust, we had to come up with a definition for eco-villages, and it seems to have hung around. 'An eco-village is human scale', that is, something where you feel that you can know the others; 'a full featured settlement', it's not just a housing development, businesses or agriculture, it's all those things; 'in which human activities are harmlessly integrated into the natural world', (I've been taken to task for the notion that humans could ever be harmless. This is an ideal and lots of biological systems exist in a relationship with the surrounding world where they are part of cyclic flows. We as humans did that during the hunter and gatherer period. We can do it again.) It's not just the relationship with the natural world that's important, it also needs to be 'supportive of healthy human development' and the sense of celebration that you're seeing here at Findhorn. Finally, we need the sustainability principle, that is a community life 'that can be successfully continued into the indefinite future', otherwise we're just borrowing from the future.

Putting this into practice we encounter what I like to describe as the eco-village challenges. I think of these as sort of building blocks. The first layer is the physical layer, biological systems: wastewater treatment, food production, animals, etc. Then the built environment: the buildings, roads, etc. These are really important parts of what an eco-village is all about, and in some ways they are perhaps the easiest parts, or at least that is the experience from those who are working these laboratories that we call eco-villages. Underneath is the human part: the economic system and the governance. If we don't get these together, we'll never effectively get the upper (biological and built-environment) level together. But in order to work out the practical economic parts, you need some kind of communal glue: spiritual, emotional, cultural, something that enables you as a community to hold together when you go over the inevitable rough spots. What winds up generating some of the rough spots—the reason I enclosed this as a whole system—is that one of the things that really catches us as we work in eco-villages is that we're doing it all at once. We're having to deal with all of these issues at the same time that there are challenges in our relationships, as our kids are needing x, y and z. This is the whole system challenge that I think often sneaks up on people and blind sides them.

To me it's an invitation to discover how to really maintain balance. One of the things about really getting into the living aspect of an eco-village is that the big ideas that you thought solved the world, all of the sudden you realise, are only part of what needs to contribute to solving the world. There's a balance that needs to happen between group and private, between what needs to happen today and tomorrow, between the hardware aspects (the buildings) and the software side (between the heart, the mind and the will. It seems to me that one of the traps that communities get into is setting up a seeming struggle between these three. For me they're another three legged stool.)

Why eco-villages? I think very simply because they are the place that most fully enable us to get at a level that allows us to grapple with the core meaning of our times. And the meaning of our times as I see it, is that we are called to be midwives to the new culture that is emerging. We can't birth culture simply within ourselves. We need to be able to do it with others, but we need to be able to do it at a scale that we can understand. I would offer you another three legged stool—our relationship with the natural world, with each other in terms of politics and social issues, and the relationship with ourselves in terms of health, personal growth and spirituality. They're all part of your larger self.

Sociologists have come up with this s-curve that they call the Diffusion of Innovations. What I've done is to take this process, this spreading of a new idea and look at how, if you want to be a change agent, if you want to be a midwife to bring some new innovation into a society, what are the strategies that you need to use? I would say that the best strategies change as you move along this curve. A lot of difficulty activists get into is that they have a great strategy but it's the wrong time. So where are we in terms of eco-villages? I would say that we've been in the Experimentation and Pilot Project territory. By experiment I mean what you get when you have these passionate, irascible eccentrics who just go out and do it. And we've learned a lot from this level, there's a lot to build on. I think it's still going on. But while the pilot projects need to continue to grow, we've moved into the stage of Infrastructure and Support Systems Building. And for the architects and planners among you I don't mean roads and electrical lines. I mean the communications infrastructure, the social infrastructure. I mean the Global Eco-Village Network and this conference. I mean

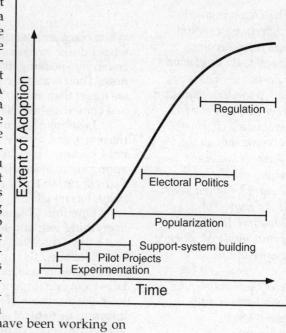

those who are working on eco-villages and who have been working on them to some extent in isolation. If we can get better contact with each other, we can speed up our own learning process and speed up the process by which we can eventually move into popularisation. One of the ways that sociologists have found to best spread ideas is to find those who are interested and motivated and help them do it better, and ignore the people who object. If innovation is something you want to block, the most effective thing to do is to go out and find the change agents and engage them in a conversation. **One of the illusions that we have gained from our notions of democracy is that nothing will change until there has been some public discussion and then there is a government action. Well folks, that is not the way that cultures are actually changing** Business know much better. They introduce products into niche markets, get them well established in the niche, let it spread from there, and have an enormous impact on cultural change. One of the reasons that electoral politics arrive fairly late on the curve is that the time to get into electoral politics is when you can win. That doesn't mean that there aren't building regulations to be changed and other political areas that need to be dealt with, but I would really encourage us to focus on the pilot projects, building up the infrastructure among us, getting in touch with people who are really interested in what we're doing, enabling the momentum to build.

I think this conference comes at a wonderfully pivotal time. We are hopefully at a point that in five years we'll be able to look back and say, 'In this conference connections were made, networks were built, understandings were developed, and a richness of celebration emerged. We learned here how to carry a certain twinkle in our eyes as we went out. And as we went back into communities where people are over-stressed, we were able to say, 'Yes, I understand all of that and there is this joy emerging through me, and lets discover together how we can bring that into being here in this neighborhood, here in this village,' or wherever it may be. We know how to grow foods that won't poison us. We know how to build buildings that won't poison us. We know how to put together pedestrian communities that will greatly reduce our need for transportation. Tap into all those things. Also, we know how to dance together. We know how to listen to each other. To the extent that we can carry that kind of energy back out into the world, I think this conference will be a magnificent seed point.

THE DYNAMIC STRUCTURE AND CONSCIOUSNESS ZONES OF HUMAN SETTLEMENTS AND THE ENVIRONMENT

Peter Dawkins

Peter Dawkins practised architecture for several years before devoting himself to the development of Zoence, or "Science of Life", a Western equivalent of Feng Shui. Peter has been leading pilgrimages and workshops on the subjects of landscape temples and the healing of the earth for fifteen years. He is a founder of Gatekeeper Trust and has recently authored, Zoence, Science of Life.

Peter Dawkins
Roses Farm House
Epwell Road
Upper Tysoe
Warwick CV35 OTN
UK

Fax +44 (0)1295 680770

00616.540@compuserve.com

When place and people come together, they can create a magic, and that's what I'd like to discuss with you this morning. Last night Peter Russell began by speaking about consciousness, particularly human consciousness. There's also the rest of nature that's conscious, too. And sometimes we forget that, and some people don't even know that. Nature is evolving and conscious just as we are.

I was involved in architecture for many years, in the normal sense of the word, and place was always very important for me. I loved the work, but I became very distressed because so often you cannot build what is appropriate, in the right site. I left the practice of architecture partly for that reason, so that I could research the effect that place, or the environment, has on us.

One thing I've discovered is that everything has a relationship to everything else and that these relationships have a very simple pattern that can be discovered. If you can grasp that pattern, which has its own consciousness, then you begin to see how your little self, in your little space, actually relates to a bigger environment, and that environment relates to an even bigger one, all in a very meaningful way. And it's possible to make a science of this, that looks at these relationships and what is appropriate to do at any time in any place. One of the phrases I like to use goes, "The secret of life is learning to do the right thing in the right place at the right time and with the right orientation." Orientation can be an outer, physical thing, how you orientate your windows, etc., or it can be an inner orientation that we all have to find.

Behind every single thing that exists, is an idea. What created our natural environment? The mountains and lakes and valleys? There are many ideas that lie behind all of that, a fantastic intelligence. I'd like to talk about this intelligence and certain things we can identify to help us work with it. Something I noticed as an architect, is that people are so affected by their environment that it can affect their behaviour drastically. What I hope will happen is that as our communities learn how to live much better with each other and the land, we will appreciate the spirit of place and come to recognise its needs and its purposes; because the land is the foundation of everything else, the vegetable and animal kingdoms. It's our home. I think when we get it right, and we have joy in the landscape, miracles occur. (Some may call them coincidences, but I reckon coincidences can be defined simply as two different realities coinciding at the same time in a meaningful way, and that's something precious.) I very much believe in the old teaching that humankind was created to be the gardener of the planet. So we must help shape the land, to make it even more beautiful. It's important to attune to the intelligence of the land and listen to it.

Our environment, our landscape, is an entity with its own life. And it allows us to participate in that life. Like us, it is composed of patterns of energy. **If you saw the landscape with different eyes (i.e. other than the physical) you'd see it as all energy. We're all energy.** We have patterns of energy, and focal points of energy which focus consciousness in us as well. We have polarity, top and bottom, and we couldn't exist without this polarity. Our manifestation occurs because of it. In the landscape you find polarity in wet and dry, hot and cold, the valleys and mountains. These polarities allow creation and manifestation to take place. In fact, it's possible to discover that the greater the polarities, the greater the potential for the creativity of that place to happen. Just as when two very different people come together and make a loving relationship, then creativity can be enormous.

Also like us, the landscape manifests places that have distinct character and purpose. We have them in our own bodies: the head is the focus of thinking; the chest of our feeling nature; and abdomen of assimilation, procreation and a will power for getting things done. It is lovely architecture that we have: a three fold architecture, manifesting the trinity of life.

Landscape is not dissimilar, and there's an art in this because once you have these three locations manifesting, then you have a seven-fold nature. In our bodies they're known as the seven focal points or chakras on the spine: crown, brow, throat, heart, solar plexus, sacral and root. This comes quite naturally from the three initial spaces, and they come from the polarity of top and bottom and the heart. And flowing between all of these areas of consciousness and purpose is energy, our very life force. If it gets blocked in us, we become ill, physically and emotionally. Landscapes can be blocked, too, through our buildings.

Sacred architecture has tried to imitate our own human structure and the structure in the landscape, As an example, in the archtypal plan of a cathedral, you can see how they tried to make a cathedral like a person lying on the ground face up to the sky. The Church calls it the 'crucifixion form'. I like to think of it as embracing the universe in love and wonder. I think it's a nicer image. You see how the nave, the main part of the building where most people sit, contains the chakras of the abdomen. Then, where the transept crosses the nave is the heart. It's the most important part of the building and of our bodies, because at that crossing is where the polarities are set up. Then up further, to the chancel, you have the choir where the throat chakra is. Beyond this is the presbytery, where the bishop sits, at the brow chakra of command and perception. The high altar is placed in the crown chakra.

There are different ways of discovering these patterns and working with them. One way is simply by instinct. Then, a step further, a certain amount of guidance comes into it, which is certainly the case with Findhorn. Chakras are manifesting wonderfully at Findhorn. There are two schemes at work here and they're placed in such a way that the head chakra of one is placed on the heart chakra of the other. This is often built into sacred architecture. It is expressed, for instance, in the icon of the Madonna and child, where the child has his head on the heart of the mother; so the head and the heart relate to each other. (Becoming in tune with yourself, or your higher nature, or as some people call it, your guardian angel, for instance, is to become aware that standing behind you is this beautiful being, and that you can just rest your head on the heart of that being. It is a beautiful thing to do. If you haven't tried it, just have a go.)

At Findhorn, the first caravan marks the first heart centre of the Community, belonging to the first chakra system which goes from north to south. The head of that first pattern is located on the Universal Hall, the solar plexus is focussed at the Community Centre, and the sacral contains the Phoenix Shop, the Findhorn Bay Caravan Park Office and the business part of the caravan park. In the root chakra is the new Living Machine.(!!) In the second pattern that is still emerging, which stretches from west to east, the Universal Hall marks the heart centre, Cullerne House and gardens lie in the throat area, and Minton House focuses the head chakras. To the east of the heart, the Nature Sanctuary and garden lies in the sacral chakra, whilst the root chakra is located in the area with the barrel houses and Bag End Cluster. It's important to recognise these things and give them respect. From what I know the placement was done through careful attunement and guidance, which is what can happen when we allow this awareness to come into our lives.

In terms of our relationship to the environment, there are certain things that are important to remember and to do. First, to attune to the spirit of the place and its purpose. Secondly, to feel how the place relates to the rest of the country and the world so we don't live in isolation, so we feel our relationship to other people and places. Thirdly, to recognise the chakras, to mark them and enhance them in the best ways possible; especially the heart centres, making sure the energy flows freely through those places. Finally, to treat our house, our village, our environment as a holy place. **If we can make it true that nature is our friend and we are nature's friend, I think we'd have a wonderful world.**

THE FINDHORN COMMUNITY   John Talbott

John Talbott has lived in the Findhorn Foundation Community for the past 15 years. He was trained as an engineer and practised in America before moving to Scotland where he thought he would become a gardener. After a week in the gardens he was asked to join the maintenance department and has been involved in maintenance and building ever since. For the past 13 years he has been coordinating the ongoing planning and building of the eco-village at Findhorn, together with the many hundreds of volunteers . He is the author of Simply Build Green, A Technical Guide to the Ecological Houses at the Findhorn Foundation. *He is currently an independent consultant and Co-Coordinated the Eco-Village Conference.*

John Talbott
Findhorn Foundation
The Park, Findhorn
Forres, Moray IV36 0TZ
Scotland

Tel +44 (0)1309 690956
Fax +44 (0)1309 691387

jtalbott@findhorn.org

I realised as I was putting this presentation together that usually I do this talk for people who are very interested in visiting a spiritual community, and I try to tell them about why eco-villages are a part of that. Today it may be the reverse. You're all here and interested in eco-villages and I'm going to tell you about Findhorn and why spiritual communities should also be a part of eco-villages. And maybe they're the same thing.

I'm going to start with the history of the Community. We've been here for thirty three years now and there has been an evolution that follows the decades. It was started in 1962 when Peter and Eileen Caddy, their three young sons, and Dorothy McLean moved into an old caravan park here on the Findhorn Bay. Funny place for an eco-village and a funny place for a spiritual community. They had been until recently successfully managing a nearby 4-star hotel. The unique part of the story is that they said they owed the success of the hotel to the following of God's guidance. This came to them in the form of Eileen's inner voice which she heard in her meditations. All three of the founders had been involved in spiritual training and were well disciplined in following what they heard in their inner voice. They were told to go to Findhorn, with their caravan where they were to wait for further instructions. They thought this was to be a temporary stop.

In the early Spring they were told to start a garden that would supply them with food and supplement their income. None of them had done any gardening before and they really struggled to get things to grow. It was the worst conditions you could imagine: pure sand here, windswept, cold, and the growing season is very short. Nevertheless, they tried.

Then Dorothy, in her meditations, began to have contact with what she called the Devas (after the Sanskrit word meaning Shining One), and she was told that they were really the intelligence behind the forms of Nature. She found that as well as containing a very pure and uplifting energy, they also contained specific information about what the plants needed and how best to grow them. So the story begins to take off here. By following these instructions, the garden began to flourish and produce phenomenal results, including forty pound cabbages and other huge vegetables. As the story began to spread, they were joined by others, including a R. Ogilvie Crombie, or "ROC", who began to have experiences with the Elemental kingdom, represented by Pan, nature spirits, fairies, and gnomes.

Despite this rather extraordinary story, it was hard to write off these quite sensible, well-educated people. There was something that was very compelling about these archetypal images that were coming through these early experiences here at Findhorn. It's something like "God is alive and well inside of you, and each of us has the opportunity and the ability to connect with that divine God within." That is exactly what Eileen was doing, and that's how she described her inner voice. The second very powerful archetype was played out by Dorothy and ROC: that Nature is alive and intelligent and willing to work with us, and 'when we're willing to work with respect we get phenomenal results'.

Really the only spiritual discipline we share here is meditation. It's not a requirement, but it's something we tend to do together, to help us explore what's going on on an inner dimension. The early community was about meditation, linking up on the inner and then doing outer work in the gardens, and a new consciousness of cooperation with Nature and spirit.

About 1970 David Spangler arrived. The community was growing rapidly, and education began to be talked about, so that we could further explore this new consciousness that we were working with. The Community Centre (CC) had been built but it was very small, there less than 30 people here. But Eileen received guidance that the CC should be expanded to seat 200 which seemed crazy at the time, but within a year there were 200 here. It was a wild and crazy time.

In 1971 Paul Hawken came and stayed for a year, and wrote *The Magic of Findhorn*, which became a best-seller and brought thousands of people to Findhorn. There was a paradigm shift where we moved from focusing on the garden and growing vegetables to focusing on growing people through the education programs. The arts flourished. We did a lot of building and working with nature. We had a lot of fun. The guest programmes really developed during the 70's and became the economic driving force behind the community. "Work is love in action" was the key note as the community grew.

By the end of the 70's, the community was over 300 people. There were 5,000 visitors a year. We had bought a lot of property, but we didn't have good financial management, and in 1979 the bank called up to say we had a 350,000 pound debt, and were nearly bankrupt. Also, Peter and Eileen split up, Peter left the community in 1979. Over half the community left within the period of a year.

There were lots of reasons for the crisis. One of them is that we weren't very well grounded. **We were working with this new consciousness of love and cooperation and having a wonderful time, but we had left out some other important things. We weren't using good common sense.**

We entered a new phase of let's be spiritual and practical. We began being energy efficient and financially responsible. The whole idea of ecology came in. The ideas that Dorothy and Roc had been exploring were mainly on an inner level. Now it was time to move that to an outer expression. It was at that time that the idea of a 'planetary' or 'eco'-village, came into being; the idea of translating these early principles of cooperation and working with nature into a built environment. In 1982 we held a conference on this theme, where the seeds began to take root. It was also hugely inspiring for us.

From being on the verge of bankruptcy and being completely disillusioned by the 70's we began to see a way forward, a purpose and mission for the community's future. We launched a fundraising drive to buy the caravan park, where we had only been renting. We were able to buy the land, and began to really develop our visions. We drew up our priorities of how we wanted to develop. We also acquired the Holiday Park business, which gave us the income to pay off the debt. Within a couple of years there was a complete turnaround. It was like a miracle for those of us who lived through it.

During the 80's we spent most of our time getting clear on what we wanted to do and consolidating the financial base. The first building that went up in the Park was the Nature Sanctuary, built by Ian Turnbull, and I think it was very symbolic that this was the first building. It is a great expression of the eco-village idea, in harmony with Nature and our relationship with Nature. We also built the Whiskey Barrel Houses, made from large recycled timber vats used in the local whisky distilleries. They are called 'spirit receivers', which we thought was very fitting for a spiritual community. Then we put up our own 75kW windmill and built a large extension for our CC, the first since Eileen's guidance expanded it in 1970. Businesses were started and the community expanded its activities to be much more village-like: a school, whole foods shop, baker, health care service, computer services and even a cafe!

By the 90's we developed a very unique system of ecological building called 'the breathing wall' based on all timber construction, and healthy and eco-friendly building materials. We have now built about 20 buildings, and with the purchase of some adjacent land next to us we will see a real spurt in building in the coming years.

Despite the physical development of the community here and how much it seems like we've accomplished, it's still a tremendously fragile place. I'm always struck by that. It never seems like we can relax. There's always a sense of being on the edge, of insecurity, not in a negative way, but just that we don't really know the future. We can't control it. And that's a key thing for me: that we need to surrender to something higher. **No matter how hard we try to make something happen or plan for it to happen, if it isn't in harmony with what is meant to happen, it's not**

going to happen. I think in our community process we need to continually go inside and do our attunements, to feel into what is right to happen next. That's a key message that I have from Findhorn, that despite all that we've done and can feel proud of, it's not all our own doing . We are playing a part in something much larger.

CRYSTAL WATERS PERMACULTURE VILLAGE
Max Lindegger

Max has been a qualified permaculture designer since 1981 and has worked on over 750 properties, including Crystal Waters Permaculture Village, and works with the development of ecological town subdivisions and villages throughout Australia. He is the co-editor of The Best of Permaculture and lives at Crystal Waters, in Queensland, Australia.

Max Lindegger
59 Crystal Waters
MS 16, Maleny 4552
Australia

Tel +61 74 944 741
Fax +61 74 944 578
ecosol@peg.apc.org

Crystal Waters is located approximately 100km north of Brisbane, in Queensland, Australia, on approximately 640 acres (259 hectares). The climate is subtropical. The Village was designed according to the principles and ethics of permaculture by Robert Tap, Geoff Young, Barry Goodman and myself. We understand a permaculture village as one that is consciously designed and maintained to optimise and balance the ecosystem of the natural environment and the people living in it.

At the moment nearly 200 people live at Crystal Waters and eventually there will be 300, that's the design capacity. We range in age from the babies to our oldest resident, who is 93. We have a great variety of businesses and occupations. Most people, because we are in a rural environment, have to bring their businesses with them, or be creative. Crystal Waters is a mixture of private and shared ownership. 14% of the total land area has been subdivided into 83 privately owned lots. A Visitors Area and the Village comprise another 6%. The remaining 80% of the land is our common and includes small lakes, areas for agricultural and horticultural development, forestry plots and bush areas. We see ourselves as an aspiring eco-village. We're not quite a baby anymore, but we're also not quite a juvenile yet either. We have a long way to go.

I don't see Crystal Waters as something which is meant to be copied. It's meant for our climate in Australia, our social and financial systems. But I think we can still learn something from examples that we can't or don't want to copy. When Robert Tap and I went to see the town planner we were told that it was a nice idea but it would be impossible for two reasons: We would not be permitted in the state of Queensland to build new villages, except if we were a mining company (and we had no intention to change and become a mining company), and the second reason was that the density permitted in a rural environment was 16 allotments. Well, both Robert and myself and about 200 other people are living now at Crystal Waters. So it seems that the impossible is sometimes possible. And I would hope that this fact would maybe inspire people who will run against brick walls and people who will say 'No you can't' and 'No you shouldn't.' And maybe it means that you have to change some laws. I think having a convict heritage (in Australia) often helps. We don't accept no for an answer.

I'd like to tell you about places that have influenced me. The village of Raza in the southern part of Switzerland has influenced me since I was a small boy, and it is still influencing me today. It has many of the elements of sustainability that we recognise today. It used the local materials, the stones cleared from the fields. It knew what its limits were. It clustered together. It had its symbol of spirituality in the centre. Its growth was limited by how much food could be grown.

But something unusual happened. While this was always in the back of my mind as the symbol of sustainability, over time, the population had dropped from 113 to 12....After the war people began drifting to the cities for work and education. The only people who were left were the old. I think what we have to learn from this example is that times will change. We have to make sure that our eco-villages will be able to cope with constant change which will come much faster . We also have to remember that we have to care for old people; not just the young and cuddly, and those in the middle who can look after themselves. We have to make sure that all of them are included in the village. I think this brings us back to what is actually enough. Do we realise what our limits are? I think we need to recognise that we have to set natural boundaries. We have to learn what the word 'enough' actually means.

Meeting places are another important part of eco-villages. In Switzerland, there were baking ovens that served as meeting places for women. As each woman would show up with a bundle of fire wood and the ingredients to bake a few loaves of bread they would talk about problems, about solutions, and there was probably a fair amount of gossip too, but gossip is important. Over the last fifty years we have been pulling down places where people can get together. We need new models. We don't need to build more bakers' ovens. But we need something to take its place.

If we separate ourselves, as townplanning often will, not only do we deny ourselves the company, we deny ourselves the wisdom of old people. When we get involved in village design, as I do, there is a tendency to forget about the people. We think much more about the infrastructure and the electricity supply, telecommunications and the roads. But we have to remember what it's actually all about. It's about people.

We have a responsibility to maintain the land we live on. With the inheritance of clean land comes the responsibility of looking after it. We have clean air and clean water, too. The Native Americans talk about seven generations. What we inherit today is from the last seven generations and we should look at what we do today as something that will be inherited by the future seven generations. I think it makes us aware as designers that we're not designing for the colour of wall paper, or colour of paint. We're talking about a place where people live, and will live, hopefully, for a very long time.

Crystal Waters makes an impact on its environment. We do create infrastructures. So we try to minimise the impact of these infrastructures. We call our roads 'access drives' because we feel language is quite important. An access drive is something more private and small scale. We built them ourselves and we maintain them.

We build structures, so we issue everyone at Crystal Waters with what we call an owners manual. We issue them with 50-60 pages of information which tells them what the thinking was behind the design. We tell them they should look at the impact they'll make with the building materials and where they come from. Does it come from a tropical or subtropical rain forest? Is it quarried nearby? Does it require a lot of heat to produce? What does it do to you when you use it? What will happen in future generations when someone has to pull down this building? Will it become a burden on a toxic waste dump or will it blend in with the earth.? We try to encourage people to fit their homes into the landscape.

In the future we hope that it will be possible to produce 70-75 % of our basic needs locally, food and vegetables. And it is happening increasingly so. I find people are building their houses, establishing a job for themselves. The gardens are being expanded. More orchards are being established. Slowly the areas between the houses are melting together. Hopefully fairly soon they will be connected by paths and useful trees producing food, forage, shade.

I feel that in our modern society it is often considered to be sufficient if we can go for a weekend drive to a park. I believe we need the connection with nature all the time. I believe we need it between our house and the letter box; our house and the children's playground; our house and where we work. I think we should be exposed, even immersed in nature all the time. And we need to also not look just at the big things, the roads and the power. We need to look at where the beauty is on a small scale too. I think that's when it becomes really fun to live in an eco-village.

I think we need to design into eco-villages what I call sacred sites. We don't have churches or a temple, we don't even have an official meditation area at Crystal Waters, but we have set aside the best land; the land which we felt that people would probably get the right feeling, the right connections from, to pray or to chant or to sing or to cry. We would like to see that nature becomes the church or the temple. If you can get the infrastructure right, and if you can learn as people to work together, and if you can find not only external success but also internal peace, then I believe the sky's the limit.

THE FARM, USA   Albert Bates

*Albert Bates joined The
Farm in the early 70's and
serves as an archivist and
community historian. He
is an environmental
attorney, gourmet mush-
room grower, and the co-
founder of the (note
spelling)*
*Ecovillage Training
Center. He is the author
of* Climate in Crisis: The
Greenhouse Effect *and*
What We Can Do, *and
four other books on
environment, energy, and
human rights.*

Albert Bates
556 Farm Rd
P.O. Box 90
Summertown
TN 38483 - 0090
USA

1 615 964 3992
1 615 964 2200
albert@gaia.org

http://
www.thefarm.org/
charities/evtc.html
*Eco-Village Training
Centre*
http://
www.thefarm.org/
mushroom
Mushroompeople
http://
www.thefarm.org/
charities/gvi.html
Global Village Institute
http://www.gaia.org/
dx/
*Home of the Design
Exchange*
(ENNA Newsletter)

Communities have a start, a middle and a finish, and there are elements of each in all phases of community. Looking at the history of The Farm over 25 years, I want to dispel some illusions about barriers to starting, because we started with virtually nothing — no money, no skills, no grand design—and by just trying, we made it happen.

In the second, or middle part, you have to balance development objectives, so that as you become more practical, and more seasoned, you don't forget why you started, or lose your idealism. The third part, the finish, is about objective criteria for judging success.

People wonder why anybody would want to enter into something as unstable and unproved as an experimental community. For me it was to join a eutopia. My children have grown up in a eutopia. And when I speak of a eutopia, I'm not using the 'u' word. I'm using the 'eu' word, eutopia. The difference is that the u-topia is no place. It's a dream, a fantasy. Eu-topia is a good place. It's achievable.

When I speak of beginnings, I'm talking about adversities, because adversities create heart. They nurture a sense of love for one another. There's an old adage from The Tibetan Book of Yoga and Secret Doctrines that says, "adversity being a teacher of the true way, is not necessarily to be avoided." Adversity builds heart.

The middle phase, the balancing of objectives, comes when we start to learn from our environment exactly where we are. The term 'sustainability' carries different meanings for different people and in different contexts. If you look at something like the Brundtland Commission Report, it defines it in a very human-centered way, "meeting the needs of the present without compromising the ability of future generations to meet their own needs." And that bears a very close similarity to the attitudes that most of us had when we started The Farm in the 70's.

The few hundred founders had come from a trip around the country and had seen wide open spaces out West. They tended to view the ecological problem as fundamentally one of greed, a misallocation of resources. But our appreciation of the problem deepened through the experiences of the 70's. We began to think in terms of whole systems of health, not merely human welfare. A whole systems approach requires a Zen balance of form and emptiness. You have to provide for form in the sense of human habitat and emptiness in the sense of human exclusion. There is no "open space" in the sense of land that is uninhabited. There are only displacements of one species by another, or, to paraphrase Stephen Gaskin, "moving protoplasm, from buffalo to beef, pigeons to people."

The needs of fellow species require understanding that we are only still arriving at. We have only recently begun examining how this rugged highland was inhabited a hundred years ago and a thousand years ago, by what kind of people, with what kind of diets and disciplines.

That evolving understanding has deepened our sense of how you relate to and and what you must confront when you define ecovillage.

Let me illustrate our experience in a little more detail now. The principal convener of our group was Stephen Gaskin, who was teaching at San Francisco State University when he started a Monday Night Class to talk about why and how young people were changing the culture they were living in. For several years Stephen taught these classes, asking, "What's happening to us, and how do we want to live? What is it that we believe in?" It was a spiritual discussion and hundreds of people who attended Monday Night Class had a deeply life-altering experience. And through that discussion a group of regular students coalesced.

Deciding to become a community, they travelled to Tennessee and bought and — 1000 acres for $70 an acre. That seems like a lot, $70,000, but if you divide that up among 320 people, it comes out to about $218 per person. There was one barn and one house on the property, and people lived at first in the old schoolbuses they arrived in. One of the first earth-sheltered solar houses on the Farm was made from a buried schoolbus.

Another early source of housing was army tents from the Korean War. We would get these for about $15. They would house 6 or more people. Eventually the flaps went up and we started putting in sides and framing and putting on tin roofs. They began to look like houses, which we called 'touses and hents.' Today some of these houses are actually quite elaborate and you can't tell they were originally tents. Occasionally you'll be walking inside a house and you'll see a little piece of canvas coming out of a wall.

A typical house that we might build today would still use a great many recycled materials. We get windows and doors from dumpsters, construction sites or landfills. **Most people send their trash to a landfill. We go to the landfill and pick up, and build houses.**

We started off with 1000 acres and added 750 acres the next year. A few of us knew something about organic farming so we started compost piles. We would muck out everybody's barn within a 15 mile radius. We would get sawdust from the sawmills. We turned large compost piles with horses. It took us about three years before we were agriculturally self-sufficient. By that time we had reached a population of about 800.

We lived for the first thirteen years on a budget of $1 per person per day. But almost the entire economy of The Farm was internal. We provided services for each other and very few of us went outside for work or to buy things. There was also very little money coming in.

We developed new and interesting recipes for vegetarian foods. Tofu, soymilk, soy burgers, soy cheesecake, soy pizzas, soy tempeh, soy yogurt, soy coffee cakes, soysage. The soybean became our strong ally. We can grow 40 bushels per acre and that fed us very well. In our tofu shop today, we make soy products we sell in supermarkets all around Tennessee and Kentucky. We're also the world's largest supplier of pure tempeh inoculate.

We had to have our own health care system because we were 40 miles from the nearest hospital. We trained our own paramedics, nurses and midwives, about 60 of them. They've now delivered over 2000 babies, mostly to people who come from outside to experience a safe form of natural childbirth. Lately we've had women doctors and gynecologists who come to have their babies with us. They know that our Cesarean rate is only 1.8%, as opposed to 25% for hospital deliveries.

Today we're looking into starting our own long distance phone company, but In the early years, we had our own phone system, called "Beatnik Bell," which reached all the houses in the community. The dial tone might be a Grateful Dead tune, or it might be a public service announcement, like more people being needed to pickle eggplant at the cannery. We also sent our own television signals out along the phone wires, so it you had a TV within 20 feet of the wire and tuned it to Channel Six, you could get our home-made evening news show. We couldn't afford to call long distance, so we would make our long distance phone calls by finding a ham radio operator in another city and do a phone patch on each end.

With our limited measure of success — developing a frugal lifestyle, growing our own food, housing ourselves with native and recycled materials, and developing our own internal business enterprises — we found ourselves having population problems. In the space of five or six years we grew from a few hundred to 1250. In any given night we might have 200 visitors. In any given week 20 or more of those people would decide they wanted to move in. We began with an open door policy and then it came to the point where we had to consider, "At what point do you say no, and why do you say no?" We began going to these visiting people and asking if anyone in the group had a piece of land, and if someone said yes, asking if that person would take the rest of the group and go start a community.

At the same time, we began having problems with our banks because around 1976 we had begun farming in a very capital intensive way. Farming commercially is a difficult proposition at best. We began borrowing money from banks for new tractors and combines and things, and then began thinking how to pay off that money. We began renting land in the winter in Florida. Well, to mechanically farm in the winter, in southern Florida, you find yourself at war with nature.

We were farming big fields and we were farming with traditional American methods, which makes your relationship to the land more remote. When we looked at what kind of soils we had created, what the land could actually support, we began to reassess scale — population on a particular piece of land, and what kind of population that land could support. We ended up pulling back from Florida and changing the zoning of The Farm.

Originally our buildings were spread all over the land. We took all the buildings and moved them into a concentrated area and let half the land go wild. One of the consequences of that is that more species came in, because they had more space. We also started farming differently because we had less land to work with. We started farming a little more intensively and began looking at hands-on, close-up kinds of farming.

Today we farm mainly through home gardens and an occasional common crop of potatoes. We contract for organic soybeans and do group purchases through a regional food cooperative.

To deal with the financial crisis brought on by capital-intensive farming, we decollectivized and divided into various different economies within The Farm. Today we're kind of like an ecology of systems. We have Mondragon-style coops, collectives, partnerships and corporations and they're all working together. Finding out how different economies can work together is part of the experiment too.

Our businesses include an electronics firm that builds Geiger counters, a book company that focuses on vegetarian cookbooks and native crafts, a mail order catalogue for mushroom growers, and a video production company. Our Ecovillage Training Center provides courses on water and energy management, permaculture, health, midwifery, and alternative building methods.

A large part of the work of The Farm today is in the non-profit sector. Many of us make a living providing services to people around the world. In that way, we haven't forgotten our original vision.

Today The Farm is a happy place to live. It's not a utopia in the sense of a perfect society. It's a eutopia in the sense of a good place.

When we look at how we've done, and how we're doing and what we need to improve, some of the objective measures are: do we have more species living on our land now than we had when we began? And we find we do. We have a lot more species than we did before, so we're managing it well. Do we have the next generation of humans wanting to continue living there? And we find that the answer to that is also yes. Our challenge is to bring the next generation into our society as full "vision partners," willing to build on what we have begun.

The Farm, or any intentional community, is not without its mistakes, calamities, disagreements, and sadness. People die, and we bury our dead and mourn their passing. Storms come, crops fail, and we go through times which are lean. Businesses fail, and the people have to pick up the pieces and start again. Times change and you have obstacles to overcome at each step of the way.

At the same time, if the hearts of the people are good, then it's still a good place for the people who are there, even in hard times. "Adversity, being a teacher of the true way, is not necessarily to be avoided." It's not the architecture; it's not the place; it's not the food; it's not the culture; it's not the lack of it. A community lives in the hearts of its people. Strong hearts make for a strong community. And strength comes from the courage to try, and to fail, and to pick yourself up and try again.

ECO-SETTLEMENTS AND URBAN RENEWAL IN EUROPE
Margrit Kennedy

I have been in the business of planning, building, renewing and researching ecological settlements for the last fifteen years and I have the feeling
that I'm just starting every time I think about it. It is a complex and de-
manding task and we have already such an incredible richness of experiences. In order to come to grips with this topic, I want to give you a brief
historic perspective. Then I want to share my dream about ecology with
you in a way I think one can do only at Findhorn. And thirdly, I will show
some eco-settlements which we have recently analysed and documented.

Ecology in Central Europe in the late 70's meant becoming aware of
the fact that we had built settlements in which the air, the water, the energy and other materials were used in linear ways. We were using them
and discarding them and the waste products were building up. The solution seemed to be to get all of these elements to work in a cyclical way,
reusing energy, water and waste, and saving materials.

Fifteen years later lots of our ecological ideas have been implemented,
some have even become standard practice in many countries of Europe.

However, what I'm going to show you is a far cry from what I actually envision ecological settlements to be. It is like the air-plane that
Leonardo Da Vinci designed — compared to today's super jets. So I'd like
to share my dream about ecology with you because I think it's important
to have a vision of where we want to go. After each part of the dream I
want to make a positive affirmation: those of you who feel that this is also
part of your dream, please, join me in this positive affirmation.

The most important part of this dream is that we will have communities which are structured in such a way that people can live complete
and fulfilling lives and that all their physical, emotional and spiritual ne-
cessities are fulfilled. And I know: 'We can do it and we will do it — and
we're doing it already.'

**The sensual part of my dream is that the very elements that we are
made up of — the fire, the water, the air, and the earth — will be an
integral part of our communities so we can be in contact with them every
day and experience their beauty.** And I know: 'We can do it, and we will
do it and we ARE doing it.'

I'm dreaming that the technologies that we are just developing will
become so simple, so refined and available to everybody, that the whole
world can afford them. This way we can make sure the planet is inhabit-
able for many generations to come. And I know: 'We can do it and will do
it and we ARE doing it.'

I dream that one day we can share our visions, in this way, everywhere. I think it is a very powerful tool for implementation if many people share a vision and affirm it on a regular basis. This way it will be
much easier to materialize our visions on a large scale. And I know: 'We
can do it, we will do it and we are doing it.'

My work in the ecological movement started for me, and for many
others, in West Berlin in 1979. In the context of the International Building
Exhibition, there were 3000 new apartments planned to be built and 3000
old apartments to be renovated. I was employed as director for energy
and ecology research. The urban structure we had to deal with was quite
bleak, and when we began our work, I thought, "if ecology can be implemented here, it can be done anywhere". Well, we have done it and are still
doing it — as you can see from the following examples.

One of the groups we worked with in Berlin was Oekotop. Their
attempts to bring life back into the city have been inspiration for most of
the urban renewal projects in Germany. This group showed, for instance,
how an old delapidated parking garage, a concrete structure built in the
1960's, could be transformed into an ecological kindergarten. Slabs were
taken out of the structure, a large glass greenhouse for plants was placed
in the middle of the building and the flat roof was turned into an open
green space. The heat that is collected in the centre of the glass roof is
brought down in ducts, stored in a heat storage wall overnight and passed

*Margrit Kennedy is an
architect and urban
planner with a Ph.D. in
Public and International
Affairs. She teaches
ecological architecture
and urban design at the
University of Hannover
and is the author of books,
articles and reports on
community, school
planning and building,
women and architecture,
urban ecology, money,
land and tax systems and
permaculture. Her book*
Interest and Inflation
Free Money —
Creating an exchange
medium that works
for everybody and
protects the Earth
*(Seva International,
Okemos, Michigan, 1995)
was a bestseller at the
conference.*

*Margrit Kennedy
Ginsterweg 4-5
31595 Steyerberg
GERMANY
+49 (0)5764 2158*

on to the rest of the building the next morning. Looking at green facades and some trees around it, the people of the neighbourhood really love this building now.

Working for the International Building Exhibition, I met experts who knew everything about energy, water, or about how to reduce garbage, green the city, and reduce noise pollution. But there were very few people who had an idea about how it all would fit together. I felt that the singular reduction of our use of energy or water was not sufficient to really create something ecological. I was looking for a more synergistic concept of ecology. One day someone told me about Bill Mollison; that he was an agriculturist from Australia who had lived with the aborigines for many years and had developed a theory on permaculture, or permanent agriculture. So we brought him to Berlin. I met him at the airport — and within half an hour, on the way back home, I had exactly what I was looking for, the key to ecological integration.

I have illustrated this key to my understanding in two diagrams in 1982. They have been used in many publications since. The first shows our present situation in the agricultural field which is typical for all of our large linear centralized supplementary systems — whether they be our electricity or heating or drinking water or sewage systems. We produce food today in very specialised systems, with an energy input to output of about 100 to 1. As a result we have soil erosion, monotonous work, unhealthy food, poisoned air and unusable wastes. This system creates chaos, hunger and death. The second shows how we can transform the current system into something permanent by making sure that every element in the system fulfils many functions and every function fulfils many elements. By adding a glass house onto your home, for instance, food can be produced without poisons, energy consumption can be reduced, water recycled, organic wastes, (which make up half of household waste) can be recycled, and a new living space can be created.

In our community in Steyerberg, Germany, it has been the most rewarding experience to actually implement these ideas. In contrast to the usual reductionist concept of ecology in Germany, where using less is associated with less quality of life, we try to show that ecology can enrich our life and make it much more beautiful. **What we want to create was something that everybody would come to and say 'Ah, this is what we want too,' and then spend their money on ecological technologies instead of gold knobs for their bathrooms.**

In the meantime, we know that ecology can work — if it is done from the grass-roots level up, if people have the power to decide what they want and how they want it. We have many models that are working beautifully. But there is not enough time for everyone to awake. Therefore, the question is: Can we impose ecology from above? Can we actually implement ecological models among people who just want a house to live in, who are not really very interested in ecology?

To answer these questions, we carried out a research project for the European Academy of the Urban Environment, in Berlin, in which we looked at examples of ecological settlement projects in six European countries. And I would like to tell you about a few examples where ecological housing has been implemented "from above" and has worked very well.

The oldest one was Puchenau, a housing settlement with 1000 units in Linz, Austria, which started thirty years ago, designed by Roland Rainer. He fought for high density development without traffic. He organised two public transit stops on either end of the settlement and saved half of the cost on sewage and roads by simply putting the houses close to each other so that the length of services was cut. By giving every house its own small private courtyard or garden, he found (on the average) that residents will leave one weekend in four to drive to a park or lesiure area, while in those multi-storied apartments without any private green space, people stay home only one weekend in four.

At Schafbruehl in Tübingen, Germany — a settlement with 111 residential units, the architects: Eble and Sambeth, have tried to take up the building forms of the old village that is next to it. The houses are built completely out of healthy building materials: bricks, wood and natural paints. The residents have space for private gardens, as well as semi-public and public green spaces. There are all kinds of corners where people can meet, children can play and community life can take place. There are places for water, too. The rain water and drainage water is led in flow forms (developed by John Wilkes and Herbert Dreiseitl) through the community. Children can play there and explore the secrets of moving water, its colours and sounds, its force and adaptability.

The Solar Village of Lykovrissi near Athens in Greece with 435 housing units is a large experimental site for 14 different combinations of passive and active solar technologies. The active solar homes have not been very successful economically, largely because the cost of energy has not risen as much as we all anticipated in the wake of the first oil crisis in the early 1970's - when the project was initiated. However, one additional learning process has been made here - so as not to be repeated elsewhere - and that is that the cost of "parasitic" energy, used for the heat pumps and for all the auxiliary regulatory devices that are needed in order to redistribute the stored solar energy, may consume as much primary energy (through electricity) as is saved through solar energy (which is thermal energy). However, the passive solar homes in contrast are a total success.

The main arguments that I hear against ecological settlements are usually economic. People always tell me it is all very beautiful, but that it doesn't pay. Back in 1982, I began to wonder why something people wanted and thought was necessary, was not possible economically. I was looking for an answer to that when I discovered something that is as basic as the need for water and food: With interest and compound interest, our money grows exponentially - which sets the stage for pathological growth of our economic system. In fact, only 3% of our present volume of money is needed, to-day, for trade or the economic exchange of goods and services. 97% is used for speculation. Therefore, with this present money system, neither social justice nor ecological sustainability can be achieved.

What we need to create is a growth pattern that allows our money system to stop growing in quantity at an optimal point in time, thus allowing our economy to start growing in quality and to increase the quality of our lives — ecologically.

Thank you very much for listening.

COMMUNITY GLUE: PEOPLE PROCESSES FOR COLLABORATION   Glen Ochre

It is lovely to be here. Everyone says that, but it's true. It is a wonderful feeling to be with 400 good people who really care about the planet. That's very energising for me, and I hope for you, too.

I'm a part of Commonground, which is a small rural commune in Victoria, Australia, which I initiated 14 years ago. We were a small group of old revolutionaries working in the welfare/community development area, and we felt there must be a better way. We asked ourselves what contribution we could make to the world. Commonground was dreamed from that question. We came up with the idea of Commonground as a resource for the social change community. It's a place where groups can come, take time out in the country, and refresh themselves.

Commonground is on 95 acres of beautiful land. We're under one roof, one table, one purse. We raise our children together. We have four children who were born into the commune and we share them. (Lots of people ask if the children know who their parents are. The answer is yes.) We are a very close-knit family. And at Commonground we don't own the land in the traditional way: we can't sell it or profit from it. That's important. No individual person can profit from Commonground. We put all our money in one bucket and went out and bought the land.

Community glue is the stuff that happens below the neck. It's a very important area and much of it's intangible. I believe very deeply

*Glen Ochre is a social
activist with a passion for
people's empowerment,
collaborative models of
living and working, and
her beloved Mother Earth.
She trained as a social
worker and has specialised
in group facilitation.*

Glen Ochre
Commonground
P.O. Box 474
Seymour
Victoria 3660
Australia

Tel +57 938257
Fax +57 938400
nonviolence@peg.apc.org

that we need models of collaborative living, and opportunities for making our own community glue in which we learn to share our resources differently. In Australia we have lots of room, so the tendency is for people to move further away from each other. I believe that we need to live more closely together. I bring you my enthusiasm for that.

I also bring you my years of experience. I'm fifty-one now. I started as a young social activist, young and idealistic. Now I'm much older and idealistic. I haven't lost a jot of it. I bring you my experience of working with lots of other groups who are doing what we're trying to do, trying to find ways of working together.

I bring you my unending optimism in our ability to find people-pathways through to sustainability, because I think we deeply want that. There seems to be in all of us a deep longing to belong and to be in balance with the environment. And we might be fearful of it. Many people come to Commonground and say "Oh, this is lovely. I think what you're doing is just beautiful. Couldn't do it myself, mind you...."

When I speak of community, I'm not meaning that people need to be a commune as we are at Commonground. But I am speaking of groups who live and work together in such a way that there is interdependence. One of the key words for me is "interdependence", that at some level we rely on each other. And "intentional" is another key word that I use in my definition of community, that we choose to be together. Community is the belonging that we all long for. We had it once and in part, we've still got it, and to me it's like we remember it. We remember it from thousands of years back. In a way we're trying to go back, for those connections and that belonging, and that gives me great hope.

I'd like us to celebrate this for a moment and do a little exercise together. Let's stand up for this. If you could connect yourself so that both your hands are connected to other hands; nobody should have a free hand. I'd like to ask you to close your eyes and just be aware of the hands you're holding. Perhaps they are the hands of strangers. Feel the texture of the hand, the temperature, the shape. Move your hand around in their hand. And yes, they are strangers' hands, and yet they're the hands of your sister or brother, and there is somewhere a deep connection that goes way back. There is a knowing. There is a longing. It's like there's a genetic memory that connects us all back through time and we've known those hands in some way since they were fins and we swam together. They are the genetic link that connects us from then to now, when our hands became limbs and we left the water. These are hands that over the thousands of years have grown and developed and have been used for such beautiful things; for gathering, for growing food, for loving, for birthing, for supporting the dying, for magic, for dancing. And in those hands, through our genetic memory, is our connectedness. And in those hands, in those precious sacred hands you hold in yours, is the wisdom, and the knowing that we need to take the world to its next stage. Just feel the preciousness and the magic of those hands. Give them a nice squeeze and open your eyes to them. And now let's sit down, gently, again.

You see, it is that connection on which I base my hope for our ability to create the people pathways that we need to bring into being the eco-villages and the new ways of living that we are so courageously building and living in now. But unfortunately, hope is not enough. It's like contraception, it's never been a very good method. It's not enough that we're good people, for I trust that we are good people. And it's not enough that we simply have good intentions, lots of groups—good people with good intentions—flounder, often with great hurt. It's not enough either that we have the practical infrastructures. The infrastructures are exciting and important, but I don't believe they're enough. We could have the perfect balance between privacy and community, permaculture, and you know, the toilet business being recycled, everything. We might have the perfect set-up, but then there's us, the imperfect humans. And I say that lovingly. Because we bring with us a great deal of baggage. We don't come into communal living pure. We bring this whole gunny sack full of stuff with us.

To begin with, we're socialised toward private ownership. Since we settled and stopped belonging to the land and the land began to belong to us, we've undergone a very profound shift. We think we have to own the land, guard it, improve it, and protect it. And so we have competition instead of cooperation. Most of us are socialised in that competitive mode. I think it's worth exploring in our hearts, the whole question of our relationship to the land. (I have this relationship with this 450 year old tree that I love dearly. In fact when I travel, I carry a photograph of it. You know when people travel, they carry photographs of their children. I carry one of this tree. And we have a very good relationship. I often think about owning this tree...what an extraordinary concept.)

Also, the way we were brought up didn't really prepare us for cooperation. We might, in our raised consciousness, have lots of good ideas about cooperation, but remember the neck business—we're not just about above the neck. It's not all about our raised consciousness. Below the neck, we carry around messages that go against sharing and cooperation. One of the things that I notice most is our disconnection from all this business below the neck. And I'm speaking particularly about feelings, never mind about sexuality. Just feelings. We learn in the prevailing culture that all that business is a bit frightening and dangerous. So we move up stairs and occupy the top floor. All the other things have to be repressed. They get relegated to the unconscious.

But we weren't born that way, were we? Children aren't like that. They're very good at expressing their feelings. What happened? I suppose the first thing is that our parents were born in the same prevailing culture as we were. But also, damaging things do happen to us, from the very profound—from war, poverty, violence, and sexual abuse—to the simple injuries that we all receive from growing in a world that doesn't honour and celebrate below the neck, our feelings, our spirit. I believe that damages us.

The child learns that feelings, and many views and opinions are not OK. They're not acceptable. People won't like you if you have them, and you'll get rejected. It seems to me that when we're little babies we're utterly dependent. So if people don't love us and look after us, we die. I believe we all carry with us a *deep* fear of that rejection. It's like a life death thing. It's that important. That's why seemingly small things can cause so much difficulty; because we're plugging into the life-death fear of rejection. And we learn that it's a good idea to keep the lid on these things.

Unfortunately, going underground with our feeling self is also our trusting, open self; the self that has the ability to reach out and make beautiful connections. It doesn't go away, but it goes underground. And so does a lot of our creative, playful and intuitive self. And we are upstairs in the lookout tower. Underground also goes a lot of our true needs and true desires. They are the deeper needs that we have learned are not good things to talk about, because they won't be met anyway. So the hidden agenda is born. People speak about hidden agendas as if they're maliciously held, and that people plot to have their hidden agendas met. Now OK, there might be some real turkeys who do that, but I think that mostly it's the dance of the unconscious. And in terms of the way we live together, we have to understand more about the dance of the unconscious.

Supposing now we're actually going to make this community glue we've been talking about. We've got the perfect set up, and there's a pot of organic soup boiling on the stove, everything's perfect, but we're going to make the glue now and mix it all together. So what do we put in it? I want to talk first about the tangible and obvious things, then I'll talk more about the stickier bits.

One of the things we need is a *Clear Philosophy*. What brings us together? Why do we want to do this? We need some sort of *Spiritual Connectedness*. *Membership* is another important question: Who are we going to share this vision with? How open is that membership going to be? We need some *Structures and Processes*. I'm speaking about structures like legal structures, joining structures, leaving structures. A lot of people don't like structures and processes, particularly us old hippies. But let's not be too frightened about them. If we make the structures, we can change the structures. We also need to know *How We're Going to Make our Decisions Together*. I often say to groups, "If you only make one decision by consensus, it should be how you're going to make decisions." We all have very naive ideas about making decisions, where we sit around in a circle holding hands. But there are lots of creative ways of using consensus-model decision making. We need to know what sort of *Expectations* we're going to have of each other. Because we all have them, whether we write them down or not, about money contribution, time contribution, and raising children. We're probably going to need some *Policies and Agreements*. How are we going to do things and make agreements? Agreements are often used by groups to protect us from conflict and protect us from having to talk to each other. **We try to have policies written to cover every contingency. It doesn't work. You're bound to have a situation that isn't covered by a contingency and you'll have to talk to each other.** So we'll need some *Processes for Dealing With Conflict*. Another thing I have a passion about is our *Connections and Relationship to the Outside World*. It was very important for me not to go off and disappear, just spinning my own muesli. **I see myself as a social activist and a revolutionary, and I always want to live that way.** So I think it's very important that we have some connection to the world. The next thing is *Courage*. And I guess that's pretty obvious. We are going to have to have courage, to work together and face the difficulties. And I don't know where you get that from, but perhaps we can manufacture it together.

Now we get down now to the more tacky bits of the glue. The first thing is our *Hearts* (you notice it's below the neck). If real change it going to take place, it has to happen in our own hearts first. I also think it is *Self Love* that will lead us to a greater tolerance of other people, because we discover that in fact, they're like us. I think that *Tolerance* and *Generosity* are essential and I mean the generosity that says, "OK, she's having a rough day today. So she did speak to me a bit roughly, but I won't go and fall in a hole about it." I think that Self *Acceptance* will lead us to a greater degree of *Forgiveness* — an important part of the tacky bit that goes into our glue. As is the *Ability To Let Go*. I don't mean to give in, I mean to let go sometimes when its important. *Listening*. We need to be able to listen to each other, and I'm speaking about listening with our hearts. Hopefully that will help us to speak from our hearts. We're also going to need *Persistence and Patience*. The *Ability to Negotiate* is important. People speak about safety in groups, and I think *Safety and Trust* come from all the other things that are in here, and the gelling of all these ingredients. We could add some *Hope*. We could add some *Optimism*, and bit of *Luck* — and let's not forget *FUN*. Because it's got to be fun, lots of parties and celebrations. Then, of course, there's *Love*, the opposite to fear, the love that comes when we fold back our fear and discover that we can connect with one another. Finally, there's that greater power, the *Collective Energy of Goodness*.

I'd like to finish by taking a gigantic step into the deep end and share a song with you. I'm not a singer, I just like to sing. It goes something like this:

> The power moves
> *The power moves*
> *through the season's turning.*
> *The power moves*
> *through the ancient learning.*
> *The power moves*
> *through the earth and sun.*
> *The power moves*
> *through everyone.*

FROM THE GLOBAL VILLAGE TO A GLOBE OF VILLAGES
Helena Norberg-Hodge

For me the eco-village movement represents one of the most hopeful and important global trends. The desire among increasing numbers of people to live in a way that is socially and spiritually rewarding, as well as ecologically sustainable, can provide the models we need for the new millennium. In fact, I'm convinced that the North will need to champion this cause as possibly the only means of averting catastrophic social and environmental breakdown. In order to understand the significance of eco-villages, however, it is essential that we examine the interrelated trends of global trade and rapid urbanisation.

Carried out through treaties such as Maastricht, GATT (Global Agreement on Tariffs and Trade), and NAFTA the globalisation of the economy constitutes nothing short of the biggest social upheaval since the industrial revolution. There are many momentous consequences to these agreements: a rise in crime, violence fundamentalism, and xenophobia; growing unemployment and poverty; loss of self-esteem, community and even democracy. Despite such pervasive and powerful changes, few people are aware of the ramifications of these arrangements. Based on the simplistic dogma that 'free trade' is good for everyone, these systemic changes—rooted in a narrow, outdated, economic paradigm—are being pushed through without the involvement of people, and often even without politicians' informed understanding about their myriad effects.

A major problem is that the global system has become so complex and so vast that very few people are able to see the outlines of it. However, understanding how the economic system works is essential in turning the tide and helping the eco-village movement to grow. Many people, particularly grassroots activists and women, shy away the minute you say "trade" or "economics". They tend to feel that these big issues are so overwhelming they can't do anything about them. Being economically literate, however, can have just the opposite effect—making us feel more empowered.

We need to look at the full picture of an expansionist system which is led by huge monopolies and is based on the idea of "comparative advantage". This theory, at the root of the notion of permanent growth, was first put forth by Adam Smith and Ricardo. The formula was, "Don't produce a whole range of products for home consumption in the local economy. We'll all be better off if we specialise and export." Up to a certain point, applying these ideas might have produced opposite results, but for nearly two hundred years industrial governments have been blindly subsidising and promoting more and more trade without stopping to reassess its impact on society or on the environment. Simply put, this process started in the colonial era when large companies like the East India Trading Company took advantage of cheap raw materials from colonies. In the early stages they were curtailed by anti-trust laws, but with time (partly aided by technological advance) these huge trading bodies grew so large that they gained monopolistic control of world trade and thereby also of national economies. These large multinational corporations have not become powerful because of conscious conspiracy on their part, but the end result of these systemic interactions is that they have outstripped individual governments in wealth and power.

These companies are behind the policies that affect our lives; in particular they have been instrumental in promoting the "Free" Trade treaties. The media is controlled by these same monopolies and it not only unquestioningly promotes the ideas which underlie globalisation but also through advertisements generates the greed that corporate profit necessitates. We are told that these treaties are bringing us together, but in fact they are increasing competition at a rate that is barely believable as well as rapidly increasing unemployment. These processes not only separate us from each other but also create and exacerbate ethnic tensions.

A certain degree of specialised production and global trade could perhaps help to raise the standard of living worldwide. But what we have

Helena Norberg-Hodge is the director of The International Society for Ecology and Culture, founding member of both the International Forum on Globalisation and Codoca (Council for the Sustainable Development of Central Asia). Since 1975 she has worked with the Ladakhi people to develop alternatives to conventional development.

For the original text or further information about the work of ISEC—including community study groups—please contact the International Society for Ecology and Culture, 21 Victoria Square, Clifton, Bristol, BS8 4ES, UK. Tel+44 (0117) 973 1575 Fax +44 (0117) 974 4853

Helena Norberg-Hodge 21 Victoria Sq. Clifton Bristol B58 4ES UK

Tel +44 117 973 1575 Fax +44 117 974 4853 isecuk@gn.apc.org

plenary sessions

failed to look at is the way our economic policies help to create and subsidise monopolies. For example, in Kenya, Dutch butter costs half as much as Kenyan Butter. Now any child would have to ask, "Is this efficient? Why is butter transported ten thousand miles?" Big business is favoured through hidden subsidies and legislative support. Taxpayers' money is going towards more trade and transport to the demise of smaller producers and businesses. In Spain, for example, though there are still many delightful markets with fresh food from relatively nearby farms, the macro trend is such that the garlic in Spain comes from China and costs half as much as Spanish garlic.

The psychological pressure to be part of the global monoculture is also psychologically very destructive. Through stereotyped role models young people in developing countries have been made to want to buy imported goods because of marketing strategy based on making people feel that 'The local is crap and imported is good.' Now women in China are having operations on their eyes to make them look more Western. In the Western world as well, women can't live up to the expectations projected by the media. We need to look at the way the global competitive economy is making us *all* feel like 'crap' by creating a sense of inadequacy.

Our lack of economic literacy makes us unaware of these links between economics and the spiritual and psychological dimension of life. I am convinced that we human beings have a longing for connection, with the earth, and with one another. This yearning and striving for connection is bubbling up in virtually every aspect of life — in the health movement, where the new direction is towards recognising the interdependence of earth, body, mind, and spirit; in architecture, where there is a trend towards relating structures to the specifics of climate and place; in agriculture, where the shift away from chemical industrial agriculture toward organic methods is increasingly promoted, even at a government level; and last, but not least, in the eco-village movement which seeks to combine all the various strands of this yearning for connection.

However, these efforts are being undermined by macroeconomic trends that not only separates producers from consumers but systematically shift rural populations into urban centres. Deeply ingrained attitudes in the West help to promote these trends. These is a tendency to believe that fast-paced urban ares are the locus of 'real' culture and diversity, while small, local communities are invariably isolated backwaters where small-mindedness and prejudice are the norm. It isn't strange that it should seem so. The whole process of industrialisation has meant a systematic removal of political and economic power from rural areas, and a concomitant loss of self-respect in rural populations. In small communities today people are often living on the periphery, while power, and even what we call 'culture' is centralised somewhere else.

Rural life in the West has been marginalised for many generations, and most Westerners thus have a highly distorted notion of what life in small communities can be. And even though much of the Third World is made up of villages, colonialism and development have left an indelible mark. In order to see what communities are like when people retain real economic power at the local level, we would have to look back — in some cases hundreds of years—before these changes occurred. I saw with my own eyes how the largely self-reliant, community-based culture of Ladakh, or 'Little Tibet', was transformed by economic development. The traditional culture was suffused with vibrancy, joy, and a tolerance of others that was clearly connected with people's sense of self-esteem and control over their own lives. Economic development, however, meant the dismantling of the local economy; and their own lives — or, in other words, it meant that local, decision-making power was shifted from the household and village to bureaucracies in distant urban centres; children were educated for a lifestyle unrelated to the local resources and alien to that of their elders; and people were suddenly bombarded with media and advertising images telling them that urban life was glamorous, exciting and important, making the life of a farmer seem backward and primitive. The consequent loss of power and self respect has led to an increase in pettiness and small-minded gossip, and to unprecedented levels of divisiveness and friction. If economic trends continue to undermine individual self-esteem and cultural vibrancy, future impressions of village life in Ladakh may soon be little different from Western stereotypes of small town life.

An equally common myth that clouds thinking about eco-villages and more human-scale rural economies is that 'there are too many people to go back to the land.' It is noteworthy that a similar skepticism does not accompany the notion of the world's population. What is too easily forgotten is that the majority of the world's people today — mostly in the Third World — *are* on the land. Ignoring them — speaking as if people are urbanised as part of the human condition — is a very dangerous misconception, one that is helping to fuel the whole process of ubrbanisation. Thus, it is considered 'utopian' to suggest a ruralisation of America's or Europe's population, while China's plans to put 440 million people in cities in the next few decades hardly raises eyebrows. This 'modernisation ' of China's economy is part of the same process that that led to unmanageably urban explosions all over the South — from Bangkok and Mexico City to Bombay, Jakarta, and Lagos. In these cities, unemployment is rampant, millions are homeless or live in slums — the social fabric is unravelling.

Even in the North, urbanisation continues. Rural communities are being steadily dismantled, their populations pushed into spreading suburbanised megalopolises. In the United States, where only 2% live on the land, farms are disappearing at the rate of 35,000 per year. It is impossible to offer that model to the rest of the world, where the majority of people earn their living as farmers. But where are the people saying, 'we are too many to move to the city'?

Instead we hear that urbanisation is necessary because of overpopulation. The implicit assumption is that centralisation is somehow more efficient and that urbanised populations use fewer resources. When we take a close look at the real costs of urbanisation in the global economy, however, we can see how far this is from the truth. Urban centres around the world are extremely resource intensive. The large-scale, centralised systems they require are almost without exception more stressful to the environment than small-scale, diversified, locally-adapted production. Food and water, building materials and energy must all be transported great distances via vast energy-consuming infrastructures; their concentrated wastes must be hauled away again in trucks and barges or incinerated at great cost to the environment. In their identical glass and steel towers with windows that never open, even air to breathe must be provided by fans, pumps, and un-renewable energy. From the most affluent sections of Paris to the slums of Calcutta, urban populations depend on transport for their food, so that every pound of food consumed is accompanied by several pounds of petroleum consumption, as well as significant amounts of pollution and waste.

What's more, these Westernised urban centres — whether in tropical Brazil, arid Egypt or sub-arctic Scandinavia — all use the same narrow range of resources while displacing more locally-adapted methods that make use of local resources, knowledge, and biological diversity. Children in Norwegian fishing villages enjoy eating cod while people on the Tibet plateau prefer their staple barley. Yet, they are increasingly encouraged to eat the *same* food. Around the world people are being pulled into a monoculture, which is levelling cultural as well as biological diversity. The urbanising global economy is thus creating artificial scarcity; by ignoring local systems of knowledge and educating children to become dependent on a highly centralised economy. The end result is disastrously high levels of unemployment, increased competition, and heightened ethnic conflict.

Precisely because there *are* so many people, a globalised economic model which can only feed, house and clothe a small minority has to be abandoned. It is becoming essential to support knowledge systems and economic models that are based on an intimate understanding of diverse regions and their unique climates, soils and resources. It is becoming essential to support the eco-village movement.

In the North, where we have for the most part been separated from the land and from each other we have large steps to take. But even in regions that are highly urbanised, it is possible to nurture a connection to place and to one another. By reweaving the fabric of smaller communities within large cities and by redirecting their economic activity toward the natural resources around them, cities can regain their regional character, become more 'livable', and less burdensome on the environment. Our task will be made easier if we support our remaining rural communities and small farmers: they are the key to rebuilding a healthy agricultural base for stronger, more diversified economics.

Many people believe that there are only two economic models— highly centralised communism and the even more centralised corporate capitalism of today. And some even tell us that, after corporate capitalism's cold war victory, 'history has ended.' However, there is a third alternative, a decentralised alternative, that would allow people—through democratic processes and responsive government—to set up the "playing field" for business. In this way the public could participate in determining what subsidies should be given and the constraints under which businesses must operate. In order to achieve this, the Maastricht and GATT treaties will have to be rewritten. If hidden subsidies could be removed, the eco-village movement would quite naturally flourish.

MY EXPERIENCE IN THE COMMUNITY: LEBENSGARTEN STEYERBERG

Declan Kennedy

The community of Lebensgarten Steyerberg started in 1984 when two brothers from Berlin who had inherited some money bought the dilapidated housing quarters of a World War II ammunition factory. Inspired by a lecture from Eileen Caddy and a visit to Findhorn, he and six others decided to create a spiritual and ecological community out of the existing row houses and various other buildings.

In May 1984, after having looked around for three years as to where we could implement a permaculture project in Germany — or some other country - we met one of the brothers, became quite enthusiastic about the place and in October 1985, we moved in and were the seventh party present. Within three years after the purchase, all the houses had been either bought or rented by people interested in participating in this community experiment. There are now about 150 persons (including 50 children) in the community - of different ages, social and professional backgrounds, and with different religions and objectives.

I would say there have been several different stages of development at Lebensgarten. First there was the pioneering stage of getting things together: finding people to live in the houses and working out amongst ourselves a plan for the future development of the site. Then we went through a time of building up and implementing our ideas. When we saw that the plans and systems we had created were working reasonably well, we began to sit back a little and feel satisfied. But then we realised our community didn't run automatically. We began working on new ideas, and late in 1994, in the context of a proposal to be part of the regional projects of the EXPO 2000 in Hannover, we decided to begin opening up and introducing ourselves to the world. As part of EXPO 2000, we plan to renovate our large hall and several other buildings, including their landscaping with water sculptures, sewage treatment and tertiary ponds.

We are often asked how the individuals and families earn their money in Lebensgarten. There are as many answers to this question as persons who live there. There is a relatively large group who are practising and teaching alternative healing methods. Another group produces arts and crafts. A seminar group organises and holds courses for subjects, ranging from encounter groups, sacred dance to practical environmental protection. There are also meditation sessions offered for a week or week-end in Zen, Vipasana, etc.

Some have created their own work, others have found jobs outside. Some individuals can carry out their free-lance profession anywhere, a few draw unemployment benefits. There are old-age pensioners, people in a transitory period who are living off their savings until they want to return to a mainstream job and a few who are making a completely new start. A couple runs our co-operative "shop" on a part-time basis. Three members make different types of jewellery. One man has started a book-store. Another has a shop for selling biological building materials. Three of the members, a computer consultant, a dance theatre producer and a physiotherapist, bake bread three times a week, for the needs of the semi-nar guests and the community. In the one room with an open fireplace, we have a cafe two afternoons per week and a "pub" on Wednesday and Saturday evenings. And many other services are offered which are linked to the people who come to participate in our seminars. About one third of the community members hold jobs outside of the community.

The experiments with permaculture in Steyerberg show that ecol-ogy is a slow and often difficult learning process and that we are now in a position to help with a wider use of the experiences of permaculture and spirituality in other eco-villages around the world. Unless we, in Ger-many (who are among the highest users of energy and other resources in the world), set a genuine example by scaling down, employing appropri-ate technologies and sustainable lifestyles, these countries will follow our destructive example.

During the past ten years, Lebensgarten Steyerberg has demonstrated and manifested some concrete examples of cultural, permacultural, eco-nomic and spiritual ways of life that help to restore the balance between our giving and taking from the earth, using passive and active solar en-ergy for heating water and for electricity for our common solar vehicle, sustainable gardening and alternative education. This is a turn towards a more simple, mindful and sustainable life style.

For the Expo 2000, we plan:
• to work out a concept for presenting the results of our work through exhibitions, seminars and tours;
• to fix up the space for these presentations by renovating our great hall;
• to offer study trips for visitors, using solar busses to transport visitors from Hannover or from the railway station of Nienburg to Steyerberg.

The most important "spiritual" maxim which has made it possible for everyone to live together in Lebensgarten is the perception that the world is our mirror. The difficulties we have with other people (or other physical, economic or social structures) always represent the difficulties which we have to overcome within ourselves. We are not victims, but fel-low-creators of our own lives. With this, we assume the full responsibility for everything we do and experience.

This spiritual outlook naturally has a whole series of practical con-sequences in respect to our daily relationships to one another and to the resources upon which we rely for sustenance. The community demon-strates to each individual that change starts within oneself and — this is consoling - everyone is experiencing similar difficulties in the process of change.

We have based our communal togetherness on the very broad ideals of Peace, Creativity and Tolerance. In an everyday situation, we are here together because we want to be. We have no central Guru, leader or reli-gious direction. According to many surveys about how communities gel and stay together, we should not be here.

We have no unified political direction, although most members would sympathise with a general green direction. We have no communal purse. We pay monthly dues to keep up the community buildings, but each per-son is responsible for her or his own economic situation.

Similar to the principle of polyculture instead of monoculture in the area of ecology, the heterogeneity in a community makes life both highly fruitful, but also sometimes difficult. Neither our up-bringing nor our sectoral education offer a good preparation for such an ecological or

Declan Kennedy is an architect, urban planner, ecologist and permaculture designer. His current projects include implementing a northern European example of permaculture, as well as designing and lecturing on eco-villages and urban ecology. Declan and his wife Margrit live and work at Lebensgarten Steyerberg, in Lower Saxony, Germany.

Declan Kennedy
Ginsterweg 4-5
31595 Steyerberg
Germany

+49 (0)5764 2158
+49 (0)5764 2368

dkennedy@lebensgarten.gaia.org

social context. This work on ourselves and within the group takes much time and energy, but is essential for the development of the Lebensgarten community.

At Lebensgarten, we try to respect and celebrate each others' differences — and that means we are continually learning a lot.

SHAPING THEIR OWN DESTINY: REVITALISING TOWNS AND VILLAGES

Jill Jordan

Jill Jordan is a community development consultant, lecturer and cultural development facilitator. She has been instrumental in setting up a number of community initiatives in Maleny, Australia, and she sees local community economic development as a preferable alternative to the current economic paradigm of large and complex institutions that are distant from the individual and the environment.

Jill Jordan
P.O. Box 87
Maleny Q4552
Australia
Tel   +61 74 943312
Fax   +61 74 943363

For more infomration on LETS, see the Resources section

I've been in the community of Maleny, which is a small town in Queensland — I'm going to say near Crystal Waters, but in fact Crystal Waters is near Maleny — for about 25 years. I'd like to give you an overview of the empowerment process that's taken place in the community of Maleny over the last twenty years or so.

The story starts in the 70's. Maleny was one of those small, dead, rural towns that exist in Australia and the rest of the settled western world, but land was cheap at the time and there was an influx of new settlers.

When we came into the town, there were many things that the town wasn't able to supply us, like whole foods. So we started to grow our own food. One evening about half a dozen of us gathered in a room — most strategies start with half a dozen people in a room — and we decided that we would start supplying some of our own needs with a whole foods cooperative. Our first business venture in the town was born. We were all overeducated, middle class, white people, and none of us had gone into business before. We wanted to buy whole foods and have an outlet for the surplus fruit and vegetables we grew. This was 1978.

The first big decision we made was that the co-op was going to be for the whole town, even though the town didn't know it at the time. **We started our first shop in one room, a pokey little place, and the locals looked on us with a great deal of suspicion. We were doing 'funny' things—as they were thought of at the time — like recycling jars and plastic bags.** But the old women of the town caught on to that. They remembered what it was like when those resources were valuable, and they would come in. At first they wouldn't buy anything, but they'd bring us their jars and bags. They saw that in fact we were selling local produce and began asking if they could sell their produce there too. More and more the locals became involved. Today that cooperative has over 650 members, 60 producers and its turnover is about $450,000 a year. It was a successful small operation and has become a successful big operation.

In 1979, Bill Mollison, who is the "mother" of permaculture, had gone to the U.S. and came back to Australia incredibly excited about the ethical investment movement. In 1983 he called about half a dozen of us into his living room in Tasmania and he urged all of us to go back to our communities and start up our own financial institutions. Because, as we were all terribly aware, access to capital is a very necessary element in actually starting up a community. Many of us were skills-rich, but we were in fact collateral poor. The banks weren't terribly impressed with us. I came back to Maleny and broached the idea at a general meeting of the Co-op, and people were very enthusiastic. So we did it. We started the Maleny Credit Union in 1984. The Credit Union is right in the heart of the town and today, services about 3000 members. It has an asset base of about $9.5 million and has put about $21 million worth of loans on land, homes, small business, etc., back into the community.

When you run a multi-million dollar financial organisation you realise that there are inherent problems with money. It doesn't matter how well you actually administer it, or how cheaply you administer it, or how small a gap you try to make between those who have money and those who don't. The rich still get richer, and the poor get poorer. At this stage, again, good old Permaculture comes to the rescue. Lea Harrison, another wonderful Permaculture teacher, was working in the US and came across Michael Linton, who had come up with a brilliant alternative economic strategy called LETS: Local Exchange Trading System (which was changed to the Local Employment Trading System, and we changed it to the Local Energy Transfer System, seeing it as being more than employment and more than trading). It is a system that allows people to trade without money. It goes back to a premise that the wealth of a community lies in its goods and services, not in its money. We now run a dual economy which supplies everybody with their needs. The wonderful things about LETS is that its not only an economic tool, its an extraordinary community rebuilding tool. In Maleny, the LETS system has 800 members and its turnover is about 25,000 units per month.

Three years after we started the Credit Union, the Wall Street crash happened. Overnight, interest rates plummeted in Australia from over 17% to less than 9%, while the Credit Union interest rates just kept plugging along at about 13%. We'd never followed the interest rates of the outside market. We had locals rush in with fistfuls of money saying, "Take our money!", and we actually turned some away. We said, "If you're interested in community reinvestment, which is where we'll put the money, into projects locally, then we'll take your money. But if you just want the highest rate of interest, you can take your money away." Some of them did. But some of them left their money, and they've become some of the biggest investors we have today.

I think the two biggest areas that people need empowerment in are the money system and our own governance. Governance impacts on us every day. Around 1991 another woman and myself were elected to Council, and that made a huge difference just in the way that the wider community of Maleny started to gain some power. When we got onto the Council we were able to introduce changes within the local community. We opened the meetings up, started public participation. It had been incredibly conservative and very closed. We also started what we called the Special Rural Task Force, which came out of a big community consultation while we were in Council, where about 180 people came together throughout the community to form a task force looking into sustainable use of rural land, not just for the people on intentional communities, but for the whole town.

During 1993 we saw the emergence of our first collective, the arts and crafts collective, which started with three crafts producers. Now there are 23. They operate a store in town with a huge range of arts and crafts. A film society was also started so that we can choose our own films in town. In 1994, we decided the time was right to start a Co-op Club. It's a licensed venue which provides good meals, where people can have a drink and listen to good live, local music. It's providing a social focus for the community. We work very hard and we also need to play very hard.

A Co-op Learning Centre has been started. Also, The Maleny Green Hills group, which has quite an interesting strategy. It was started by the professional and business people in the town, after the Council went back to business as usual after the last elections — which meant development at all costs. This group of people got together and said 'We don't want this'. The community has become so empowered that it has formed a Trust Fund so that the community can actually put money aside and buy significant pieces of land that they won't have the local government develop.

I think you can see that we now have a community that knows what it wants and knows how to get what it wants—that's the most important thing. There's a momentum in Maleny now. The skill building that has taken place has allowed more and more people to start the organisations. We started with the basics; with food and money, then land, shelter and energy, then people producing their own income and finally culture, communication and education. You see this process among people who start their own communities. It's been a very organic process in Maleny, I believe.

What I'd like to say to you is that it's not just Maleny where this kind of thing can happen. Maleny is a special place, but so is every other community. We've realised that although all our strategies are different, the elements are same. They are replicable, across the world. First, the elements for the strategy must come from a need, a communal need. It doesn't matter how good the strategy is, if it's not a need of the community, it won't take off. You also need someone to mother a strategy. You need midwives, too, but you also need someone who will hold the focus while it's in its infancy stages. Next, don't overreach. It's better to have a small success than a huge failure. If we start small and sustainable, we will always be sustainable. Finally, skill building is important. This is not only the technical skills, the administrative and financial, but most importantly, the interpersonal skills; learning how to help people make powerful decisions and resolve conflict. When you get a few people together you will have conflict. If you run away from it, organisations will never prosper.

I want to talk a little bit about the politics of embedding these strategies within the wider community, because it's very different, revitalising towns and villages, from bringing up 'green field' sites, as we call them. Basically, when we first arrived in Maleny we were incredibly confrontational with the old settlers there. We were so rude. We saw the farmers as enemies. We castigated them because they misused the land. We didn't allow that they were doing the best they knew how. We didn't realise how fearful they were of losing their livelihoods. And basically we presented a threat to that livelihood when we came in.

In the old ethic, there are two groups of people: there are the people who tell others what to do and there are the people who are told what to do. But empowerment is about making everyone responsible for their decisions. This is diametrically opposed to the old way of doing things and no wonder it's threatening. It's important for us to realise — and this is my growing point at the moment and I'm getting better and better at it — where that fear comes from and work with that. Work with the fear, acknowledge it, and find a strategy that can overcome it.

Just a few techniques to do this that I've learned... Provide a lot of information. Be open and leave space for people to change their minds. Enlist peoples' skills. The local saw mill is a great consultant for local tree planting projects, for example. There are very few people, that if you go to them, and say, "I need some help", won't open themselves to you and provide that help. Fear is always broken down by familiarity and understanding.

I'd like to talk about the problems we've had with growth. When you've got a vibrant community, it's like moths being drawn to a flame. We have an 8.5% per annum growth rate in Maleny. It's huge. It produces social problems, especially with the older people because they feel very dislocated when they walk down the street and don't know anyone. As people flood into an area, only about 30% of the people who come in as labour force are able to be accommodated with jobs in construction, retail and commercial development that happens as a result of the growth. There's another 70% of people who we have to assist in actually growing their own jobs. It's also important for us to remain open as a community and provide opportunities for people to join in.

Now, we have people who actually come from other parts of Australia to learn about our community on the ground and take it back to their own communities. The message I bring to you is that the process you've heard about is entirely replicable everywhere in the world and it is entirely appropriate that it happens. Every community is unique, has its skills and its diversity. It's our duty to actually empower our own communities in their own special ways and encourage that uniqueness.

WHAT IF? BUILDING AN ECO-SUSTAINABLE EARTH ECONOMY
Guy Dauncey

*Author's Note : The original presentation told the story of the birth of a sustainable earth-economy in the Moray Firth Region of Scotland over the years 1995 - 2015, in a fictional mode. The paper was impossible to reduce to 3 pages without losing its historical flow. This is an abridged summary of the key components of the journey. The components are described in more detail in the author's After the Crash : The Emergence of the Rainbow Economy *(3rd Edition, Greenprint, London, 1996).**

Guy Dauncey lives in Victoria, British Columbia, Canada, where he works as an author (writing a major eco-novel about the next millennium) and as a consultant/activist in the field of sustainable community development. He is author of After the Crash: the Emergence of the Rainbow Economy. *(Greenprint, 3rd edition January 1996).*

Guy Dauncey
2069 Kings Road
Victoria, BC
CANADA V8R 2P6
Tel +1 604.592.4473
Fax +1 604.592.4473
gdauncey@islandnet.com

1. Understanding the Dilemma

Everything has to start somewhere - even the building of a sustainable earth economy.

"Never doubt that a small group of thoughtful, concerned citizens can change the world. Indeed, it's the only thing that ever has". (Margaret Mead).

So — a group gets together, and they spend 6 months learning everything they can about the state of the world's economy and ecology, about signs of progress towards sustainability. Their findings ?

"First, things are far worse than we thought they were", they said. "Our economy, while it has delivered many truly good things to us, is fundamentally hostile to Nature in the way it operates. Almost without exception, each act of economic growth is accompanied by an equivalent act of ecological loss. From Nature's perspective, the economy is behaving rather like an alien organism that is preying on the Earth in a parasitic feeding frenzy. It takes what it needs, without any understanding of the ecology or the context, spews its wastes into the air, soil and water, and dumps the final debris."

"At a profound level", they continued, "the solution lies with a substitution of intelligence for matter, a decoupling of economic growth from associated growth in the input of material resources. The Rocky Mountain Institute in Colorado and the Wuppertal Institute in Germany are saying that we should build a 'Factor Ten economy', that is ten times more efficient in its use of energy and raw materials. In so doing we will both strengthen our economies, and make them more sustainable, ecologically."

The Sustainability Curves indicate the shift we need to make. Curve A shows the typical exponential growth of Earth's economy as it heads towards the limits of Earth's ecological existence, its rendezvous with disaster. Curve B shows how this growth really consists of two curves, one representing our ever-growing consumption of material resources, the other the growth of embodied intelligence through science, engineering, and the development of social and cultural wealth. Curve C shows how our consumption of material resources must be rapidly turned around and stabilized, while the curve of intelligence, which is also the curve of spiritual and invisible wealth, can continue to grow, since it is not bounded by any physical limits.

Curve A

Curve B

Curve C

All over the world, people are working to change the way the economy works so that it performs in harmony with nature, instead of hostility. There are initiatives being developed in governments, businesses and banks, communities and households, farms, forests and international agencies. The economy cannot be 'fixed' by economists, or any other kind of specialist. It is the expression of an interconnected, cultural wholeness, with links to our food, energy, houses, communities, values and our own children, as well as our businesses and trading relations. Throughout this wholeness, a massive turnaround is in process.

2. Decoupling - Closing the Loop — Industrial Ecology

On a physical level, this means building the linkages so that our economies function as an organic part of nature, so that every waste becomes a resource and all spare energy is recycled back into work, not the atmosphere. In 1992, California set up Recycling Market Development Zones (RMDZ), and Oakland and Berkeley set up a joint zone to establish strong connections between recyclers and enterprises using recycled feedstock, closing the materials-use loop. By November 1995 the zone had helped create 155 new jobs in businesses using recycled materials, while diverting over 100,000 tons of material from landfills. In Kalundborg, Denmark, over 15 years, a group of adjoining industries (including a coal-fired power plant, a refinery, a plaster-board factory, a pharmaceutical factory and the city of Kalundborg itself) have been building a system of industrial ecology, modeling nature by using each other's waste materials.

3. The Greening of Every Business

Wherever a business is active, it has a relationship with the Earth. Every business, large or small, needs to undertake the process of greening. This is easier when you group together to help each other. In Vermont, the 265 members of Vermont Businesses for Social Responsibility (9,000 employees, over $1 billion collective turnover) educate and learn from each other, assist each other with environmental initiatives, and work to achieve progressive social and environmental legislation in Vermont.

4. Green Plans — Integrated, Comprehensive, Long-Term Planning

There's no escaping it - the issues are complicated, and for the most part, we address them in separate boxes. A country which has broken away from this trap of organizational reductionism is Holland, which introduced its Green Plan in 1989. The Plan takes a 50 year perspective, and works closely with business in key sectors of the economy using goals, indicators and four-yearly progress reports in areas such as pesticide use, carbon dioxide emissions, wildlife habitat protection and recycling. They are currently embarking on their 2nd 4-year plan. New Zealand is also making progressive moves in the same direction.

5. Reducing C02 Emissions

The 2500 scientists of the Intergovernmental Panel on Climate Change (IPCC) are saying that we need an 80% reduction in greenhouse gas emissions if we want to stabilize the process of climate change. If you set up a Task Force and asked them to raid the world's supply of CO2 reduction strategies, these are some of the solutions they would bring back to you : Legislation to encourage a high standard of energy efficiency and insulation; one-stop shopping retrofit partnerships involving local companies, energy utilities and banks; energy bonds to finance investments into solar, wind and other renewable forms of energy; mandatory trip reduction programs for larger employers; true cost parking, to reflect the real cost of land; networks of cross-country trails for cycling, hiking and horse-riding; annual passes for the local bus services pre-paid out of local taxes; feebates (fuel-inefficient cars pay extra tax, efficient cars pay less); electronic road-pricing; additional taxes on the price of gas/petrol, using the income to support public transit; using a 'CO2 Profile' to measure the CO2 impact of different urban designs; car-sharing co-operatives, telecommuting.

6. Sharing the Work

Meanwhile, 10% or more of the working population is unable to work — and very few are enjoying it. **Studies from economists show that with a 4 day-week or 8-day fortnight productivity would rise, employers' con-**

tributions for national insurance could be eliminated and average pay need be only 5% less. In Denmark, the government Sabbatical Leave Scheme was such a success that the hospitals ran short of nurses and some day-care centres had to close as parents took their children back home. The pressure for worksharing will only come when unemployed people themselves pick up the placards and start picketing the workplaces.

7. Community Trusts

Worksharing may remedy the central ailment, but it will still leave numerous communities mired in poverty and alienation from years of prolonged unemployment. It will need the widespread adoption of Community Trusts to tackle this, taking their spirit from the movement for community economic development that began in the 1970s, and the community businesses that flourished in Scotland the '80s and '90s. The Trusts need to be given control over government budgets for local welfare, unemployment benefits and training, to combine with their local economic development work. With these powers, and by using community banks, local currencies and sustainable technologies to build local trade, they will be able to rebuild shattered communities. It is a work that will need many years.

8. Local Food Production

We are heading into a global food crisis, triggered by China's economic growth. Families who get by on low incomes or depend on welfare cheques will see their money disappear in front of their eyes, their children crying with hunger. Organic agriculture and permaculture farmers will pick up their hoes; local communities will convert streets and waste lands to grow food; roof gardens will blossom; seeds will be collected and shared.

9. New Technologies

Technology has such an important role to play in this overall change. Renewable energy; energy efficient technologies; living machine (solar aquatic) sewage treatment; the rapid expansion of Internetworking; electronic community databases; new lightweight materials; recycling technologies; recyclable building materials; solar-voltaic roofing tiles; ground-source heat pumps.

10. Green Investment for a Green Earth

Do you know where your pension or savings are being invested ? Are they supporting the growth or the death of nature, and community ? This is where community banks, credit unions, socially responsible investments, peer-lending schemes and a variety of other eco-financial systems are needed.

11. Ecological Taxation

This means thinking differently about what constitutes 'wealth', and measuring it differently, too. Hazel Henderson's 'Country Futures Indicators' are one good example : there is so much more to true wealth and prosperity than the accumulation of things and the expenditure of money. We also need to be placing heavy taxes on our use of natural resources such as energy, water, timber and wastes, while reducing taxes on incomes and jobs. This gives important price signals to the market, and shifts our priorities.

12. Watershed Stewardship Councils

Meanwhile, we must not forget the land itself, along with the water, mountains, valleys, and the winged, four-legged, crawling and standing-still creatures that live there. Stewardship Councils enable all the stakeholders to work together to protect and sustain the watershed (or eco-region) as a whole.

13. Containing the Global Corporations

Meanwhile, too, many multinational corporations are behaving with the impunity of pirates, blackmailing governments, buying politicians, relocating their offices, minimizing taxes and spending millions to get laws reversed, all in the name of increased profits and share-values. **The value of small, local eco-initiatives might seem like a gnat's pee, compared with the ecological holocaust being practiced by corporations around the world.** In the USA, community groups are starting to challenge the charters granted by state jurisdictions which give 'criminal' corporations their legal existence. What kind of legislation would encourage responsible corporate conduct ? A state-based Social, Environmental and Employee Responsibility Act, offered tax-incentives to corporations which adopt a package of reform measures including worksharing, telecommuting, employee-shareholding, public environmental and social auditing, community directors, and a ceiling on executive salaries ? A UN Global Code of Social and Environmental Conduct, enforceable at the International Court of Justice in the Hague ?

14. Building an Eco-Sustainable World Economy

'The corporations represent just one aspect of the overall confusion that rules at the global level. It sometimes seems that the entire world economy has been set up to encourage grab-it-while-you-can economic greed and ecological piracy. **On any day of the year, $1 trillion (a thousand billion) is traded in 'virtual securities' — derivatives and future options on stocks, bonds, commodities and currencies.** Not a cent of that money supports any actual business, farm or forest' (from After the Crash). We have developed local and national democracies, along with economic controls, but we stand at the brink of developing a true global democracy, with the benefits, taxes and constraints involved. The tiniest (0.003%) of taxes on international currency speculation would bring in $8.4 billion, about the same as the entire UN budget. Taxes could also be charged on the use of international airspace, and international waters. Over the next 20 years, it is essential that we rein in our global economic piracy, which, whether wittingly or unwittingly, is destroying the ecology of the Earth.

15. Voluntary Simplicity

Finally, the list of components comes back to ourselves. Are we really living the way we want to ? Could we live more simply, and trade less pay for more fulfilment, less quantity for more quality ? The voluntary simplicity movement started in an organized way in the Seattle area of the USA, building on a vague spiritual desire some people had to get back to a simpler, less consumer-heavy lifestyle. By careful financial planning, increasing numbers of people are able to live more simply, giving their new found time in service to the local neighbourhood, or to the Earth. Which is where, at the end of the day, it all begins !

PAUL WINTER CONCERT

Paul Winter's musical realm has long embraced the traditions of many of the world's cultures as well as the extraordinary voices from what he refers to as "the greater symphony of the Earth", including wolves, whales, eagles, and several dozen other species of "wilderness musicians".

At the Conference, Paul played pieces from several of his albums, including: "Lullaby for the Humpback Whale and Mother", "On the River", "Northfork Wolves in the Midnight Rain", "Wolf Eyes" (dedicated to the reintroduction of the wolf into Scotland, in which the audience joined together in one gigantic howl), and "Sun Singer".

"The village vision over the years has explored how we can unlock our own expression in the context of making music together in nature. Several times I've taken groups to Baja, the Grand Canyon. We invite everyone to participate. It has nothing to do with musical experience or the groundless notion of talent. It's about the music that's in everyone and your own song, whether it's a musical song or something that grows into a metaphor for you own life path and vision. Several times, at my farm in Connecticut, I've held Living Music Villages for a week at a time. The group includes beginners and amateurs who think they have no music in them, to full tilt symphonic musicians who've never improvised and want to find a way past the printed page. The idea of these kind of processes relating to the village work that all of you are exploring is exciting to me.

To that end, I am interested in finding ways for music to serve your work and the cause of bringing our wayward species back to the earth and back to our instincts, to continue on the path of maturation as a species."

Paul Winter
PO. Box 72
Litchfield CT0675

Tel +1 203 567 8796
Fax +1 303 567 4276

pwnclmr@aol.com

The concert ended with the audience singing a song from the Commonground Village at the Rio Conference in 1992:

> *In a circle of friends,*
> *In a circle of sound,*
> *All our voices will blend,*
> *When we touch commonground.*

THE TECHNOLOGICAL FOUNDATIONS OF
ECO-VILLAGES   John Todd

I dedicate this talk to artists, in particular to Paul Winter and to Haydn Stubbings, the extraordinary painter who created the panels in The Universal Hall. I also want to honour the paths from which I draw: green architecture and green materials; renewable energy research and development; systems theory and analysis; biological and organic agriculture; biodynamics; ecological landscape design; eco-forestry; space colony research; restoration biology; ecological economics; permaculture; traditions, or the old ways; advanced materials development; biospherics, or Gaian research; and Taoism.

There has been a new field emerging over the last two decades called ecological engineering, which is beginning to reach technological maturity, and which can provide some of the technological foundations for communities. For twenty-five years I have been searching for instructions from the natural world, the kind that exist in a pond or a forest. Out of this search has come a set of instructions and patterns that allow us designers to begin to formulate technologies that are symbiotic and supportive of the natural world, and serve humanity. The scientific foundations for these technologies are rooted in ecology, evolutionary biology, natural history, and engineering — gossamer engineering in particular. When taken together, we can begin to see the foundations of a new family of technologies which are called living machines.

What is a living machine? The majority of its parts are alive. They're made up of thousands of different species from the microscopic realm, higher plants, vertebrates, and so on; all brought together for a specific purpose, to serve human needs. An ecological designer takes forms from the natural world, puts them in a contained space, and asks them to do something; grow foods, generate fuels, or treat wastes. It is possible to design living technologies that have the same capabilities as natural systems do — self-design, self-repair, reproduction, and self organisation in relation to changes — functions that now take technological society inordinate amounts of chemicals, materials, and energy, often with harmful environmental consequences.

Underlying the design is a series of twelve quite coherent principles. Their importance is that by following them, anyone can begin to design a living machine to carry out useful work. I can't go into detail in such a short talk, but the December 1995 edition of *Annals of the Earth* covers them in detail.

The first living machine was the Microcosm in 1970. The goal was to create a self-contained environment that would provide food for a small group of people, using design intelligence from the natural world, without recourse to fossil fuel use, in a 10m geodesic dome. The geodesic dome provided a climatic envelope that let in light, and retained heat, and created a climate independent of the rugged New England winters. As the design was modelling the Earth's environment, the majority of the floor surface area was water. The water and land area were farmed using life forms that supported the ecosystems and provided human food. Mirror carp, for example, stir up the bottom sediments, preventing anoxic sediments from accumulating, and are edible. The system worked extremely well, providing food throughout the year.

The next stage was the Cape Cod Ark. It was created as a multi-levelled structure with different types of crops, passive solar design, and a wind engine. In the back were tall, water filled cylinders. And when

John Todd is a biologist who has pioneered the use of ecosystems as a form of technology, otherwise known as Living Machines, for purposes including the treatment of wastes, purifying water, and food production. He co-founded the New Alchemy Institute, with Nancy Jack Todd, to create science and practice based upon ecological concepts. John is the first biologist ever to receive the Chrysler Award for Innovations in Design, in 1994.

John Todd
1 Locust St.
Falmouth, MA 025440
USA

Tel +1 508 540 6812
jtodd@igc.apc.org

they were filled with algae, they absorbed enough radiant energy from the sun to heat the building. The plant life on the surface of the water gained their nutrients from the fish waste; micro-organisms on the roots of the plants transform the toxic fish wastes into available nitrogen for the plants.

Going on from this, we began to think of a new kind of architecture: solar powered barns that one could live in, linked to many kinds of ecological cycles. The result was The Ark on Prince Edward Island. The whole building is computerised, controlled with sensors. It is one of the earliest buildings to use advanced computer technology to try to understand its metabolism. Living in that structure, warm in the middle of a snow storm in January, you get a sense of how it might be possible to live in wildish lands, without destroying the environment around you.

Another area we've experimented with is in treating poisonous waste. One pond in Massachusetts was so badly damaged that it lost the ability to metabolise it's own dying organisms. To heal the pond a floating living machine was built, using wind and solar power to pump water over fluidised beds. Over three years the living machine has processed 20,000 cubic metres, in particular removing the ammonia, which is poisonous in water. The pond has become alive again. The quality of water determines the quality of life. Without water there would be no life.

What we are trying to do with living machines is shrink the need for human beings to impinge upon the natural world by several orders of magnitude. It is possible that we could reduce our impact as a species on global systems by 90%, to help create an era when human beings and nature live in symbiotic harmony, in which wildness spreads daily.

THE UNSEEN INFRASTRUCTURE OF COMMUNITY   Nancy Jack Todd

I begin by honouring Findhorn, and especially Eileen Caddy. Truly you are the cornerstone of what is going to bring us along as dwellers on this planet.

I don't really belong to an eco-community. I live more on a bridge between what could be and what is. I have friends who have grown up in community, and have spent most of their adult lives trying to recreate the experience. People need to have a sense of belonging, of community. I have a community, only right now it's global; a global tribe. One of my major heroes is Laurens van der Post, who talked about the recognition that we all have of each other, that we are all neighbours. We are all part of the human race.

What binds us as an emergent tribe, a universal people, is a sense of what is wrong. As Wendell Berry said, "How can we take care of other creatures, all born, like ourselves, from the world's miraculous fecundity, if we have forsaken the qualities and culture that inform the natures of children? We (North Americans) are conducting a sort of generational warfare against children." This is unsustainable.

On the positive side there is a shared vision. There is a world view of Gaia, that great and sacred biosphere being, which informs all that we do. Equally strong is our passionate commitment to justice, to equity, to understanding, to all humanity, to the sacredness of all life, and our passionate determination, and our optimism.

So, at this point in time, it is a question of human identity and destiny, and of our place on Earth and beyond. Scientific foundations for our shared spiritual view are being built — by Teilhard de Chardin, Thomas Berry, Fritjof Capra, Peter Russell.

Many people now want to learn, or remember, who they are. A Native American woman at the New Alchemy Institute said that a blade of grass, a seed, a flower, unfolds according to the instructions it has been given. Native Americans try to live according to their instructions. She

Nancy Jack Todd
1 Locust St.
Falmouth,MA 025440
USA

Tel   +1 508 540 6812

didn't understand what our instructions are. And at the time I could only say to her that we've forgotten. I think we're finding them now. I think we're involved in a very profound search for our instructions, and some of them are coming clear to us. Through the New Alchemy Institute, through the peace movement, through instructions from the natural world, and through the women's movement. **There is a desperate need for the emergence of women in key decision making positions; a profound need for the reemergence of the feminine, balanced component of all life.**

Ecological design has the potential to be as profound a change as the explosion of electronic communication. And beauty, our love for the world, needs to be incorporated into our ecological design and eco-villages.

I think we are in the process of rediscovering Taoism. I understand the Tao as being the Way, the great way of nature, the great way of being. It was believed that by taking a receptive and yielding attitude toward the natural, the Taoist would gain an understanding of the larger world. To act according to one's deepest, truest self was to be simultaneously in harmony with nature and with a larger mind.

And finally, I'd like to share a conversation from the New Alchemy Institute. First person: "All the fishponds and so on are so superficial; all it really is about is love." Second person, in reply: "Yes, but there is a difference between theoretical and applied love."

Nancy Jack Todd has been active in the environmental movement for more than twenty years. She is vice-president of Ocean Arks International, where she edits its publication, Annals of the Earth. She was also a co-founder of The New Alchemy Institute. She and her husband, John Todd, have co-authored many books, including From Eco-Cities to Living Machines: Principles of Ecological Design. She is currently working in a book about women and ecology, called Daughters of the Earth.

THE AUROVILLE COMMUNITY
Alan Herbert and Marti Mueller

Alan Herbert began the presentation:
On February 28th 1968, Auroville was inaugurated by 5000 people; dignitaries, UNESCO representatives, and young people from 126 countries and all the Indian states. The young people put the soil that they had brought with them into a marble urn in the geographical centre of the community-to-be, as a symbol of a place where people could live and work in harmony.

Then they all went home, leaving behind the 10-12 people who had colonised the land. Auroville is located on a sandy plateau 100 miles south of Madras in southern India. When the community began, the land had been extensively deforested and overgrazed. The fragile topsoil was eroding catastrophically, gouging canyons into the rock-like laterite that lay underneath. To survive, the first Aurovillians had little choice but to concentrate on healing the land; by preventing water runoff, planting trees, and putting up fences to protect it from grazing. There was an incredible idealism on one hand, and on the other, a very harsh and irreducible reality. These two polarities are very true of Auroville. During the first decade and beyond, most people who came to Auroville became involved in this land work.

Auroville holds the vision that beneath the surface there is a deeper, truer, reality, which can assign to each individual his or her true place, harmonise discord, and prepare humanity for the next great step in evolution. Sri Aurobindo said: "Present humanity is not the apex, but a transitional stage in a continual ongoing process of evolution, and is therefore inherently unsustainable in it's present form. Even as the animal man has been largely converted into a mentalised, and at the top, a highly mentalised, humanity. So too an evolution or conversion of the present type of humanity into a spiritualised humanity is the need of the race."

Auroville's growth and development can be divided into four periods:
1. To November 1973. The Mother, who provided the vision and inspiration for Auroville, lived in Pondicherry, 6 miles away. Major decisions were usually referred to the Mother. It was the pioneering period. She died in November 1973.
2. Following the death of the Mother, there was a dispute over who should run Auroville. An organisation in Pondicherry that had raised the money,

Alan Herbert has lived in Auroville for fifteen years. He spent his first years there involved in tree-planting and land restoration work. Today, he is the coordinator of the Auroville Communication Centre and involved in running courses on a sustainable future for professionals, students, and NGO's from all over India.

Alan Herbert
"Samriddhi"
Auroville
Tamil Nadu
India

+91 413 62341
+91 413 62274

75757.2546@compuserve.com

and, under Indian law, actually had their names on the land documents, decided that they wanted to control the project. This created tensions with the people living in Auroville, who were doing the physical work of creating the community. This escalated, becoming a physically violent conflict. The Aurovillians had to ask the Indian government to come in, so that they would have a chance to develop the community according to the ideals that they had.

3. In 1980 the Indian government came in and took over temporarily. The following decade was a period of growth and consolidation. Many initiatives were started; education, schools, cultural activities, renewable energy, health services, village development and empowerment.

4. The 1990's. Having created a stable base within the community, the orientation has now changed to interacting with the wider world.

Auroville is a place of incredible diversity. We are a community of 1100 people from 35 countries, of whom the local Indian population are the most numerous, spread over 1100 acres. The land is divided up into a number of blocks by village land and government land. **Auroville is very much a working community, rather than a place of presentation.**

How does Auroville measure up as an eco-village? Our achievements include:
• The land work: over 2 million trees planted; control of water run off and soil erosion; organic farming and gardening.
• Alternative energy: 160kW of solar voltaic panels installed; biogas plants used and manufactured; 30-35 windmills; and grey water recycling.
• Building technologies: developed techniques using compressed earth blocks, and produced the powerful presses to create the blocks.
• Development of the villages.
• Health care, including body work.

Institutionally Auroville belongs to nobody. We can build there, we can put our houses there, but it all belongs to the community. It is very decentralised.

What is unsustainable about Auroville? Transport: there are lots of cars and motorcycles. The housing situation: we are building individual houses, and there are fewer collective eating places than there used to be. The community grows only a small proportion of the food that it needs. The people are more likely to work for an export orientated small business than on the land.

Why is there so much that is unsustainable? The human diversity of the community itself creates a tremendously diverse pool of ideas and talents. It is very strong in terms of individual initiatives and very weak at the centre. Newcomers find themselves a place to live and to work, but there is no kind of process in learning the language and culture of the community.

Auroville has been described as a failure, because there is no real unity and plenty of conflict. But positively, beyond the conflicts, people can get to the stage of learning something. When the ideals are brought into reality, the psychological and social patterns brought from the old world reappear. If it is possible to step back when we get to the point when we are blocked, to surrender and be open to the input of a larger intelligence, then we can really go places. Eco-villages shouldn't become ego-villages. We are challenged to keep introducing the sand into the oyster, and to see that any kind of growth is going to come out of the unexpected. What makes Auroville sustainable is the diversity, and that we are willing to let go and let a larger intelligence take over.

Marti Mueller:
I want to open by saying 'namaste' to you. Namaste is a Hindi word meaning 'I acknowledge the Divine in you.' **It is no accident that Auroville is in India, where there is a tradition of deep love and respect for nature.** But the modern context is that India is in a state of crisis. In the next 10-12 years the population will double. There is an exodus from the rural areas to the cities; 1000 people arrive in Bombay daily. The land is desertified, as a consequence of deforestation, and agriculture is no longer considered an honourable profession by Western-influenced youth.

Sri Aurobindo was an Indian yogi, philosopher, poet, and revolutionary, who was imprisoned by the English. In prison, he saw that his way forward was in a spiritual direction. He saw man as a transitional being, on the verge of coming into an age when a new species would be created, with a higher consciousness. The Mother started to manifest the new consciousness in a practical way. She had a vision for Auroville: that there should be some place on Earth that didn't belong to nations, that belonged to no one in particular, but to humanity as a whole.

Auroville is a community that learns from the wider world, for example from Findhorn people about group consciousness. Auroville also contributes to the wider world through practical reforestation projects, alternative technology, aiding Tibetan refugee settlements, and the Earth Restoration Corps, which is a major project to restore the environment using unemployed young people.

I'd like to end with a quote from Sri Aurobindo: "The sense of the impossible, is the beginning of all possibility."

Marti Mueller
81 Rue de Temple
75003 Paris
France
+33 (1) 42 58 20 76

THE CENTRE FOR ALTERNATIVE TECHNOLOGY   Peter Harper

Peter Harper is a biologist, gardener and landscape designer who has worked at the Centre for Alternative Technology since 1983. He also writes on many green issues and is the author of
The Natural
Garden Book.
He is mildly obsessed by compost.

(*Peter began by showing the introductory video seen by visitors to the Centre for Alternative Technology, started in 1974 near Machynlleth in mid-Wales*).

The older Ecovillages contain a precious fund of experience, and I would like to summarise some of ours. I am addressing particularly those who are just starting up - although I'm sure the old lags will find much to make them smile.

First, what worked for us? Certain technical things are easy to reproduce by following 'recipes', and are increasingly common in environmental bodies:
• Renewable electricity supply: wind, water and sun with a diesel fuel backup, giving 90% renewables and excellent reliability.
• Ecological building: using environmentally-sound materials and very low energy consumption, down to 10% of typical levels.
• Biological waste treatment: all solid and liquid waste treated, with 90 % nutrient recovery.
• Recycling of glass, metal, paper and some plastics.
• Sustainable land-use: no agrochemicals, minimum intervention, habitat creation - leading to far higher biological diversity than surrounding land in spite of rapid development and intense human activity.

That was technical stuff. Many of our organisational patterns too, are normal among mature 'alternative' organisations:
• Flexible, democratic structure, owned and managed by its members.
• Management largely decentralised to individuals and departments, with an elected co-ordinating group.
• Equal wages for all permanent members.
• Most decisions by consensus, with provision for voting by secret ballot if absolutely necessary.

Peter Harper
Machynlleth
Powys
SY20 9AZ
Wales

Tel +44 (0)1654 702400
Fax +44 (0)1654 702782

Centre for Alternative Technology   http: //
www.foe.co.uk/CAT

These are all important elements in the quest for sustainability, yet in isolation they have little value. They must be amplified: they must get out into the world and propagate themselves. At the same time an ecovillage must be economically self-supporting. One of the most important and unusual things we have done at CAT is to develop activities which simultaneously get the message across and provide an income. They include:
• A visitor demonstration centre with 80,000 day-visitors a year.
• Innovative residential courses on a wide range of 'green' subjects, at various levels, for up to 40 people at a time.
• Information and consultancy service.
• Publications focussing on detailed information and practical solutions: 80 titles currently in print.

The organisation has survived, grown, spawned several independent enterprises, and has an annual turnover of more than £1 million. Success? In many directions, certainly, but let me now wipe the smug smile off our face by turning to the far more interesting topic of failure. There are many areas where we have not achieved what we originally hoped, or have even slipped back:

• Communal life: has declined, to the extent that 'ecovillage' is no longer an accurate description. There is little interest in classical communitarian living, and most of the staff now live off the site,

• Transport: there are a lot of cars in the car park, and rather fewer bikes in the rack. A definite black mark here.

• General eco-hypocrisy: do we always use organic veggies, eco-cleaners and paints etc at twice the price and half the performance, as we urge others to do? On the whole we do not, except for token efforts if someone else is paying.

• Local affairs: our global perspective means we tend to ignore local matters and have not integrated very well with the local population

• Maintenance: The place always looks a bit scruffy; we are good at initiating things, not so good at maintaining them.

• People care: individually there's a lot of solidarity and affection, but we have not institutionalised it very well.

• Finances and fundraising: although we're still here, it's always a struggle and we always seem to be broke.

• Accurate eco-auditing: progress rumbles on with rough-and-read assessments, but in spite of our avowed purpose we are not always sure whether our results are valid or even moving in the right direction.

• The spiritual dimension: is probably hiding under a bush somewhere, but I haven't found it yet. The organisation is rather aggressively secular!

One may well ask why we have succeeded so well in some areas and failed so dismally in others. I am not sure, but perhaps some light will be shed by the next list, which asks, what have we learned? How have we changed? In some ways it is a catalogue of revisionism: new organisations setting out on the same path should ponder this list.

• We take a much longer view now. In the early seventies I remember thinking we had perhaps five or ten years to Save the Planet. We were in such a panic! Twenty years later things remain urgent but we realise they cannot be changed overnight. Now we're thinking in terms of fifty or a hundred years.

• Once we thought that modern society was terminally corrupt and we should have nothing to do with it; that we should be as self-sufficient as possible. Now we see ourselves as inevitably part of both British and global society and want to participate in and change it. We have moved from withdrawal to engagement, and regard self-sufficiency as a quaint hobby.

• As a corollary to this, we have accepted that we are modern people. We have somehow to achieve sustainability but we do not want to be peasants, and there will be no 'going back'. Once upon a time we thought the future lay in a sophisticated kind of neo-primitivism. No longer.

• We also accept that most of the action is going to be in the cities, where most people will be living and where, contrary to our original arcadian assumptions, sustainable modern lifestyles are more easiy achieved. Farming, as always, will have a crucial part to play, but will not figure prominently in most people's lives.

• Many famous and groovy-sounding eco-techniques turn out to be ineffective in practice, while others which seem dull and ordinary really deliver the goods. Technologically, it is important not be deceived by appearances.

• We recognise now that collective, shared, large-scale systems are sometimes the right solution and give the best ecological answers. Small is not always beautiful. It may well be the first thing to try, but don't apply it dogmatically.

•There is no substitute for numerical accuracy. Without it you can easily be out by a factor of 10 or even 100 and be going precisely in the wrong direction. You must do the numbers.

• We have learned that reality does not necessarily speak for itself. At the beginning we thought people would come along and look at our work and say, "Wow, that's fantastic! I'm going to do it too!" No. They don't. If they notice it at all in its raw state they usually get the wrong end of the stick. Ideas, principles, structures, equipment, all have to be presented in the right way to command attention and understanding. Presentation is vital.

• Skills are precious and take time to develop in individuals. The process can be inhibited by too many changes of job or compulsory task rotations.

• Consensus-based decision-making by the whole group is inefficient and soon becomes tiresome. We now accept the necessity of an elected management team to deal with the larger issues.

• In earlier days we thought we had all the answers. Now we know this is pathetically false, and that we must play our part in the wide sustainability movement. It is useful to develop maps of the movement, the better to know who is doing what, and where our most useful contributions may lie.

Perhaps these lists reveal us for what we are: ageing bourgeois greenies who have acquired a stake in mainstream society and don't wish to rock the boat too much! But perhaps we have a role to play as a source of reliable information, and a bridge between the mainstream and the more radical parts of our movement. Sustainable systems are invariably mixtures of hardware and software, and ecovillages, unafraid of lifestyle changes, will be the laboratories of techno-social innovation that we need so urgently for our voyage into the 21st century.

THE SPIRIT OF CITY UNCONCEALED
Clare Cooper-Marcus

Findhorn is my home away from home; I lived here with my two children in the mid-eighties. It is wonderful to be back, contributing in this way. I'm going to be talking about another leg of that three legged stool, that is how to make cities more socially and spiritually supportive of their residents. I'll start with a brief look at history, to suggest where we are in our cities today, why we have a problem and how we might make cities more socially sustainable.

Not so very long ago in the industrialized West, we were living in villages in large extended families. And while the village was probably not as idyllic as we imagine, there was undoubtedly a lot of social contact. With the Industrial Revolution people moved to cities, worked long hours, and lived in cramped conditions. The street became the centre of community life. Then, as cities got more and more dense and prosperous, there arose a middle class. The notion emerged, in the West at least, that the city is bad and nature is good. This is the so called Anglo-Saxon pastoral ideal, or in the U.S. the anti-city movement. To "protect" the women and children, middle class wage earners moved away from the supposed evils of the city into leafy suburbs, and the cult of domesticity began. This led later to the garden city movement which spread from England all over the world, eventually to the sprawling suburbs of today. It reached its peak in North America in the 50's and 60's, with the explosion of low density suburban development dependent on cars and freeways around our major metropolitan areas.

Since then we have seen the rise of what we might call alienation in the contemporary city. In many North American suburbs the streets are empty, there are no sidewalks for walking and garage doors dominate the landscape. Social commentators have remarked on the unhealthy imbalance between public and private life. Recent surveys in the US show that membership in traditional communal structures like churches and parent teacher associations is falling, while shyness is on the rise—not something you particularly associate with Americans—but people are beginning to lose the ability to engage in casual encounters with a neighbour, or to reach out to each other.

Clare Cooper Marcus is a Professor in the departments of Architecture and Landscape Architecture at the University of California, Berkeley. Her areas of interest include: medium density housing, children's environments, design guidelines, healing environments, and the psychological meanings of home and garden. She is the author of Housing as if People Mattered: Site Design Guidelines for Medium-Density Family Housing *(with Wendy Sarkissian: University of California Press, 1986) and* People Places: Design Guidelines for Urban Open Space *(with Carolyn Francis: Van Nostrand Reinhold, 1990). Her latest book is* House as a Mirror of Self: Exploring the Deeper Meaning of Home *(Berkeley, Conari Press, 1995).*

Clare Cooper Marcus
2721 Stuart Street
Berkeley, CA 94705
USA

Tel +1 510 548 2904

In barely 150 years we have gone from a primarily public life in our villages and early cities to a primarily private life. How can we begin to look at the design of our cities and recreate them to be more socially supportive, more neighbourly? One solution has been called the 'soft edge' by Jan Gehl, an eminent Danish urban designer. Soft edges are features which project out from the house into the public domain, softening the demarcation line between private and public space. It can be something as simple as a set of steps or a porch where people can sit outside, smile at their neighbours, or tend to their plants.

A second solution is to slow down traffic. A study in San Francisco showed that people living on heavily-trafficked streets regard as home territory only their own house or apartment, while those living on streets with light traffic tend to see the whole street as their home territory. If we can slow down traffic, and set policies for "traffic calming", we can create settings where people may begin to know each other better. In this regard, one of the most exciting innovations is the Dutch notion of the 'woonerf,' translated as 'residential precinct,' which creates a street where the distinction between street and sidewalk disappears. While the addition of special parking, trees and street furniture, cars are forced to travel at low speeds, giving the street back to pedestrians and children playing.

A third solution to a more socially supportive city is to increase densities. We need to look more closely at forms of medium density housing in the city where clusters of slightly smaller apartments and housing units are balanced by the provision of shared outdoor space. St. Francis Square, an urban co-op in downtown San Francisco, is a very successful example. The landscape architect was on the design team right from the beginning, assisting in a site plan that made a green oasis in the city, around which the three-storey housing is clustered. There is a constant waiting list of people who want to move there, suggesting that the solution for some people is not to live out in the country or the suburbs, but to live in the city in a setting that is supportive of children and community life. With more people *living* in cities, more mixed land use, the viability of public transport and of street life are both enhanced.

We also need to enrich public life and the design of public places. The contemporary experience in U.S. cities is that once you create a public place that is attractive and well designed—a plaza or roof garden in a downtown office district, for example—people come out in droves to use it. I find it interesting that while we're touting the information superhighway and creating global connections between people, public spaces in cities are buzzing with people who are hungry for face to face socialising. Such resting and meeting places need to be inviting to all types of user groups: office workers, mothers who might be at home and not meeting each other, elderly people, children, teenagers and people with disabilities.

I think we also need to look at a whole continuum of housing choices, from eco-villages to intentional communities to urban coops to communes. Cohousing is one interesting contemporary solution. The fragmentation of communal life, long commutes, busy lifestyles and increased distance from old friends and extended families are causing many people to look for a different kind of home and social milieu. The advantages of cohousing in which each household has a complete unit but shares facilities in a common house include: more social contacts; grassroots decision making; shared work, cooking and child care; economic savings—meals are less costly, energy costs are lower; and a safer environment for children.

You've been shown a lot of images and received a lot of information this week. So now I'd like you to close your eyes. Get comfortable and focus on your breath. Imagine walking somewhere on a beautiful day. You see a figure coming towards you... You see it is a child... Now you see it is yourself as a child, and you meet. This child wants to take you to a place that was very special to you when you were young. Explore it now in your imagination, touch it, smell it. What does it look like?... What are its boundaries?... Is anyone there with you?... What are your feelings in this place?... Now turn to your neighbour and share this experience for a few minutes.

You might want to think of doing this exercise with a group who is trying to create cohousing, or a participatory planning group, in order to begin to understand and share your environmental roots and values. How many people remembered outdoor places? *(Most everyone raises their hands.)* Invariably people remember outdoor places. Since for most of us, the age-period of 5-10 years was when we started to explore away from home on our own and gain a valuable sense of independence. It is also helpful to write your own environmental autobiography, describing places that are still with you, still touching you, good and bad. Also try drawing your own *ideal* environment. This is a wonderful technique for exploring your visions of the future. Or you can draw an image of your feelings about where you now live, and then conduct a dialogue between yourself and your house. Imagine talking to the house as if it were animate. When I use this technique in interviews I suggest people start by saying, 'House, the way I feel about you is...' Then after a while, I suggest they switch roles and become the house speaking back. You'd be surprised what your house might have to say to you! Some people speak more honestly as the house, than when speaking as themselves.

Another method I've used to help people understand their spiritual connection to the environment is to ask them, "Think of a time when you were very upset, confused, or stressed, and you went some *place* that helped you to feel better. Where did you go? What was it like? What did you feel there?" It's no surprise that most people said they went out into nature. People want to go where there was sensory stimulation; it seems to wake us up out of our grief or unhappiness. One man described the importance of clouds and the weather. "The qualities which touched my mood were the views, specifically the enormous expanse of sky and cloud patterns. I felt very small and in a physical and metaphysical way felt insignificant in the universe. This made my problems seem less burdensome. I could accept that they too were transient. " Water, too, was often mentioned when people were seeking spiritual and psychological solace. People also sought what I call private places in public settings, places where they could be alone but still had visual contact with other people. Some people went to view points which helped them to "get things into perspective".

The process that people seem to follow is that of a journey to a place where they are awakened by some kind of sensory stimulation; this triggers a return to their centre, the mood of grief or confusion gradually disappearing; and finally, people experience some kind of expansion into a higher state of consciousness. Interestingly, this same sequence of movement to a place, centring and consciousness-expansion is also what we do when we meditate.

Health, holy and wholeness all come from the same root. When we recover a sense of wholeness or reconnection with our soul we are healed both physically and psychologically.

We need places in our cities for social support, but we also need places to be alone, to be with ourselves. We need places where office workers can go and be in contact with nature. Even just a few minutes can reduce stress levels. In preparing for this talk, I asked friends what *they* would do to make our cities more spiritually sustainable. Most people said they'd like a neighbourhood place where they could go. Not a church, but a sort of community centre, with outdoor space where they could meditate quietly or meet with friends and share their spiritual lives together. What they described was a kind of sanctuary.

What else would make a city spiritually sustainable? We need to unconceal the physical roots of the city. In Berkeley, California, where I live, many of our creeks are covered up and flow through pipes and culverts. Now there is a successful movement to "daylight" those creeks. We need to bring nature back into our cities in the form of parks and green spaces along natural water courses. We need to ensure that our children have access to the primary elements of our planet. So that the next generation is ecologically literate and prepared to protect the environment. A British politician recently vowed that he'd ensure that every child would have access to a computer. Better that he'd vowed that every child would have access to nature and sturdy boots in which to go

The alternative plenary session —
Peter Vallance telling a story in the tepee

Alan Watson Featherstone planting a tree and a
second generation Findhorn resident; his son Kevin.
5 ceremonial trees were planted on Findhorn's newly
purchased 5 acres during the tree planting ceremony;
participants were asked to bring a small natural stone
from their local area to contribute to the ceremony.

Margrit Kennedy coining
what became the
conference mantra:

"We can do it,
we will do it,
and we ARE doing it."

Lama Yeshe of the Samyê Ling
Tibetan Buddhist Centre opens the
Living Machine with a blessing for
long life and good luck

Jonathon Porritt reminding us to look outwards in our work

John Talbott lights a candle during the opening ceremony in the Universal Hall. The Hall was filled to overflowing for the ceremony which acknowledged each of the 40 nations represented as well the nature kingdoms and Gaia, and included indigenous music from around the world

The Humla doorway served as the entrance way to the field where the tree planting ceremony took place. It was built as a gift from the Moray community to be the entrance to a new health clinic in the remote Humla region of Nepal. Initials of project donors were carved on the back. The Nepal Trust, a Findhorn based charity, organized a trek to take the doorway to Humla and help build the health clinic.

Diane Gilman and John Talbott, conference co-ordinators

exploring. Don't let's get carried away with virtual reality when true reality — particularly in the form of the natural environment — is crying out for out attention.

As Wendell Berry, a wonderful American writer, poet and philosopher has written: "And the world can not be discovered by a journey of miles, no matter how long. But only by a spiritual journey of one inch, very arduous and humbling and joyful, by which we arrive at the ground of our feet and learn to be at home."

Finally I'd like to read you a poem. Please take the hand of the person next to you and close your eyes. I chose this poem before I arrived here but I think it connects wonderfully with one of the most moving pieces that Paul Winter played the other evening, interweaving his music with the honking of geese. The poem is called "Wild Geese," by the American poet, Mary Oliver.

"You do not have to be good
You do not have to walk on your knees
for a hundred miles through the desert, repenting.
You only have to let the soft animal of your body love what it loves.
Tell me about despair, yours, and I will tell you mine.
Meanwhile the world goes on.
Meanwhile the sun and the clear pebbles of the rain
are moving across the landscapes,
over the prairies and the deep trees,
the mountains and the rivers.
Meanwhile the wild geese, high in the clean blue air,
are heading home again.
Whoever you are, no matter how lonely,
the world offers itself to your imagination,
calls to you like the wild geese, harsh and exciting—
over and over announcing your place
in the family of things."

REGENERATIVE COMMUNITY DEVELOPMENT Bob Berkebile

This for me has already been a remarkable gathering of spirit. While it's been said before, I'd like to repeat it because it can't be said too often,how much we all appreciate what Diane and John, and the community have made possible for us during this week. Thank you.

What I'd like to do is share some of the questions that have come up for me so far this week. I believe, as Teilhard de Chardin did, that "The future is in our hands." These questions that keep coming up for me, relate to that belief. I would ask you to consider them and help me with the answers.

I was part of a very interesting conversation last night at dinner. We talked a lot about sludge. Some felt that we can deal with sludge in a physical way, like with John Todd's Living Machines. But someone suggested that we have much more trouble with the psychological sludge. And maybe we need to find a way to clear that. Maybe we are all a little constipated in our eco-communties and in our communities in general and in this conference so far. So I'm raising these questions so that we can help each other clear away the sludge.

My first question has to do with these terms we continue to use. We've talked about sustainability a lot, and eco-villages. And I wonder if those words aren't very limited. Peter Ellyard, a futurist, raised the point that sustainable implies just surviving. We need to think about thriving. What is it we're trying to sustain? Is it what we have today on this planet or is it something else? We've talked about eco-villages. It is a useful term because it narrows it down to something. But it's a little exclusive. We tend to be isolationist. A lot of our communities when they were founded, were very different. There was a natural separation between those on the inside, and those on the outside. But that was a long time ago. The world has changed dramatically. I'd like to submit that the rest of the world is changing a lot more rapidly than we are in this spiritual community. Maybe it's time to consider that and see what's in store for us in the future.

It's really important to be clear, and be honest with each other even when it hurts. It's better to challenge in love, to admit when we are hitting a wall, tripping over a barrier, uncomfortable. Some of the things I've heard being talked about, either I haven't quite agreed with or it hasn't felt right in my gut and my heart. I believe that the world is changing today at the most frightening speed. We know the planet is growing at the rate of 250,000 a day. How do we in this spiritual eco-village relate to that kind of situation, to the 5.8 billion people on this planet? If there are 400 of us here, and if each of us represents 500 other people who are not here, that is 200,000 people. That's less than the increase in daily population on the planet. We are 1/3000 of 1% of the world's population. We're not perfect, we don't have it all right yet, but maybe this planet doesn't have the luxury of us arriving at perfection. Maybe it's time for us to take the best we have and start reaching out into these communities outside Findhorn. Maybe it's time for us to act like the water hyacinth, with 27 miles of roots.

If you look at nature, all the exchange, all the activity takes place at the connections between things; at the connection between the sea and the land, the forest and the meadow, the earth and the sky. In those zones is where all the change takes place. If we stay in these walled, isolated, out-on-the-edge eco-villages, there's not much exchange. I think this may be a time when that exchange is critical to human life on this planet.

We've heard alot about the in-migration. I'd like to share what is happening in my own community in Kansas City, Missouri. For three decades now Kansas City has experienced dramatic migrations in two directions. The population in rural communities has been moving in toward the edge of the city in search of jobs, while others are moving from the core to the edge to escape crime and other perceived problems. Suburbia sees most of the growth. At the same time, the core of the city has experienced more investment from CorporateAmerica. But from the core of the city to the suburbs, the population and economic vitality have declined every year for thirty years. So the centre of the city is dying but for a few blocks of huge buildings. The edge of the city is growing like wildfire and quality of life is declining dramatically both in the core and at the edge. If I look at the future, I believe that in-migration will start reversing, people will start moving back out, away from failing core cities and edge cities.

I've heard us, and myself, talk about 'THEY', the big corporations, the ugly government. What I'm feeling sitting here is, that's me. 'THEY' in this case, is me. Now I have been on this journey for a much shorter time than many of you, and I have seen incredible change. Some of the big ugly corporations gave me the most support when I was trying to change the construction industry in the US. I think you would be amazed if you start talking with 'THEM'. I guarantee that in them is the same damage that Glen Ochre talked about. All those corporate executives and elected officials are in the same boat. Spirit is in their soul, in their bodies, trying to get out. We have the opportunity to invite them to release that. And I guarantee you that they are very capable people. They will give us a level of energy and vitality that we could desperately use. I think the planet could use that kind of vitality.

In the projects we have been sharing there is a tendency to seek a beautiful place and to create a village in that beautiful place. But if you look at our landscape on this planet what you will find is that we have degraded it. We can no longer accept just diminishing the impact of our design decisions, structure decisions and site selections. We must restore with every decision, with every act. And if that's true, we have to think about working within those cities that are collapsing, within those existing neighbourhoods, making a city attractive enough that people will stay and not out-migrate.

I heard conversations following the presentations last night (Peter Harper, Alan Herbert and Marti Mueller) where people said how

Bob Berkebile specialises in restorative architecture and is the founder of the American Institute of Architects' Committee on the Environment. He believes that a more holistic approach to planning and community building can improve the economic and social vitality of communities, as well as restoring the environment.

Bob Berkebile
1200 Main Steet,
Suite 1515
Kansas City
Missouri 64105
USA

+1 816 474 6910

b.berkebile@bnim.com

plenary sessions

important it was to focus on the spiritual centre and then grow from there. I agree with that. But again, that sounds very isolated to me. If we are a spiritual community, does that mean we cannot be environmentally sustainable? It seems to me that is a requirement. If we are a spiritual community, we must be restoring the environment. That is part of spirituality, it seems to me. I don't think there's any question in any scientist's mind that the world is dying beneath our feet. If it is not a spiritual community taking the lead in that, then who? If it's not you, and all the communities you represent, there's not much hope for our children.

Finally, when Nancy was speaking yesterday, I wasn't connecting with what she was saying somehow. But she woke me up with beauty and with love. Something we are in desperate need of is more beauty and more love, and expressing it in our communities, in what we build. There are some nice examples of that here at Findhorn, starting with the Universal Hall, in the detail even of the stonework outside. But what about the rest of the community? Does this express the spirituality of this community? I don't think so. And people on the outside certainly don't think so from what I can tell. Shouldn't we be creating something, that when you walk in, it takes your breath away? Every object that we create should in some way demonstrate spirit. Winston Churchill said, "We shape our dwellings, and afterwards our dwellings shape our lives." I'm an architect, and so I look at things in that physical way. That isn't the whole story, but that is a critical part. We have to be creating an environment, with the land and the buildings, so that the exchange between all of these elements is integrated into a whole, is nature, celebrates nature, touches our heart, lifts our spirits .

There's a wonderful story about a man in Los Angeles whose backyard was entirely fenced, so he couldn't see into his neighbours' yards. And he became curious about what his neighbours were doing in their yards. So one weekend he and a friend got some helium balloons and attached them to his lawnchair. He got a can of beer and a little pellet gun, so he could shoot the pellets at the balloons when he was ready to come down, and they released the chair. But they miscalculated. There were too many helium balloons and instead of floating up slowly, he shot up rapidly to about 3000 feet. He dropped his beer, and he dropped his gun, and was just hanging on to the chair when the air controllers saw this thing on the radar screen. They started notifying the pilots about an unidentified flying object. One of the pilots radioed back and said the UFO was really a guy in a lawn chair. This guy in a lawn chair was desperate to make a connection. And I think you can help him make a connection.

I think this kind of thinking was most clear in 1942 when Einstein was so stunned that his science had created such a destructive weapon. He told us a couple of things: "We shall require substantially a new manner of thinking if humankind is to survive;" and " We can't solve any problem at the same level of consciousness that created it." That's what I want to talk to you about.

We are surrounded by signs and people and suffering and fear that suggest that it is time to change course. But we are so busy doing what we do, we have so much inertia that we're hanging on to our course. We really have to look at our present cities and existing neighbournoods. The real question is how can these issues inform us about places like Findhorn and the eco-village that is envisioned here? What are the opportunities for restoring this site, for making this area of housing as beautiful as the forest, for making each of the buildings as intentional and careful as the one where we are (Universal Hall)? Can we introduce that same spirit in our cities?

If we really care about our children, I think we need to recognise that what Einstein said is important. We need a new consciousness to make this change and I think you represent that consciousness. We have to be more clever, more aggressive, more honest with ourselves, to get rid of the sludge.

As you leave, I'd like you to decide what it is that you can do that is more than what you came here intending to do, to change your community, to convert yourself, to really make a difference. Bring that decision back with you tomorrow and John and Diane will give us the chance to put our decisions down on a piece of paper. Today as you leave there will be clay at each of the exits which will be made into a vessel to hold your commitment. Touch this clay. Leave your energy on it. This clay will become a part of the new eco-village here at Findhorn and the future of this place.

Now if we can stand up before we go and take the hand of the person next to you, I think we need to be bold, and listen to that voice within and know what spirit is and not be too frightened of what the future is. All we have to do is see the next step. So close your eyes. I'd like you to repeat after me "I am a being of light. I am making a difference. I can do more and I will do more."

Antonella Verdiani

UNESCO (The United Nations Educational, Scientific and Cultural Organisation), beyond speaking for it's 180 member states, is now attempting to listen to and to advise communities at the grassroots level, by creating new programmes, like the one I'm going to introduce to you this evening.

Environmental education and sustainable development have been an integral part of the action carried out by UNESCO for many years. **One of the fundamental purposes of UNESCO is to serve as a link in the realm of ideas, knowledge and commitments.** The Planet Society was formed to create an international exchange network in these areas. The network is open to individuals, schools, communities, municipalities, companies, universities, institutions, the media and so on.

These people and organisations can create and develop what we call "New Projects for Living", each of which has the intention of promoting and preserving the natural environment, or the social and cultural heritage of the community that they are a part of. They can use the network to exchange ideas and resources, find partners, financial backing, technical advice, or new opportunities. To communicate, the Planet Society uses radio, television, newspapers and the information superhighway. The exchange market is the way of bringing the resources offered, and the resources requested, together. The Planet Society Review is a magazine, which will be distributed by the most prestigious newspapers in the world, reaching millions of people. The language and the artwork of the magazine is aimed particularly at young people, but without detracting from it's universal appeal.

I would now like to talk about the campaign which we call "The World Is Still In The Making", which is a part of the Planet Society program. The purpose of this campaign is to awaken in a new generation a greater sense of awareness about the future of our planet, and to give birth to New Projects for Living. It is aimed at children and young people in order to encourage them to imagine an original action, to be carried out within the framework of schools, with the help of teachers. Since the beginning of the last school year, 30,000 children in 35 countries across the world have become involved in the experimental phase of this campaign.

Antonella Verdiani trained in architecture and as a town planner, and now works with UNESCO. After spending time in Senegal and various other African states, she became aware of the importance of the grassroots level of communication. She sees her work with UNESCO as an opportunity for communication to take place between individuals and organisations cross-culturally.

AntonellaVerdiani
Planet Society – Unesco
1, rue Miollis
75015 Paris
France
Tel +33 1 45 68 45 95
Fax +33 1 45 66 06 62

Rashmi Mayur

Rashmi Mayur is the president of the Global Futures Network, based in Bombay, and is widely travelled author and lecturer on sustainability issues. He is advisor to Wally N'Dow, Secretary General of the Second United Nations Conference on Human Settlements, to be held in Istanbul 5-14 June 1996.

The planet is our habitat, it is our home, but it is now totally fouled. There is no sense in developing small eco-village projects alone in the developed North, the real question is how we are going to make the whole planet sustainable, otherwise this project or that project is not going to make a difference.

Today there are 5.8 billion people on the planet. What habitat is there for these people? 48% of people on the planet are urbanised. 1.3 billion people on the planet do not have homes, they live in shanty towns, with 9 people to a little shack made of tin and plastic. How do we provide for all these millions of people who are migrating into the cities? Today, 1.2 billion people have a food intake of 1,000–1,500 calories a day, when we need to have at least 2,500 calories. Where are we going to get the resources to take care of them?

It may look to you that these are almost impossible problems, and we are tempted to say that the problem is for the Third World to sort out. But today it is a globalised world, in every way. When the biodiversity disappears, the species disappear for the whole world. For the last 300 years we have believed that we are the masters of the Earth; we can exploit it the way we want it. But we are now realising that this is wrong. We are a part of the Earth, and must protect the Earth. And many of us who are struggling to realise that if my child is going to have a decent place to live I want every Third World child to have a decent place to live. Our whole philosophy should be based on the reverence for life, wherever it is.

In the Indian epic called the *Mahabharata*, Arjuna has 150 soldiers, and is confronted with 10,000 enemies. He asks Krishna, the god, how he could fight with any prospect of winning against all these enemies. Krishna says that the important thing is to fight the war against evil, not whether you win or lose. And our task is to carry on the war against evil, against the technology that is destroying, against human beings who have become heartless, and against the destruction of the environment.

Robert Mueller

The aim of my talk is to give a framework within which this conference and its activities are developing. In my 40 years in the UN, I have seen 3 very basic changes.

From 1945-70 the UN was focused on humanism and humans; on avoiding war and preventing children dying, and on The Declaration of Human Rights. The Charter of The UN does not mention the earth. Why? Because in our belief the Earth was limitless. This continued until the late 60's, when advanced countries like Sweden and people like Rachel Carson had begun to notice that something was wrong with the environment.

A completely new period of history started with the First World Conference on the Environment in Sweden in 1972. There was a continuation of the preoccupation with humans, but also preoccupation with the world around us. It was only in the late 60's that we realised that we had a population problem, because the fertility rate continued at about the same level, even though the mortality rate was declining. The population explosion intensified the problem of the environment. In 1980 we began to get warnings from climatologists that something was going wrong with the world's climate.

The result is that since 1980 we have entered a third period - from now on the earth is number one, and humanity is number two. Humanity is number two because we wish humans to decline on this planet. And we have begun to ask about the consumption of resources by Western developed countries which is 30 times the amount for developing countries. Believing that the world was unlimited, we started with the discipline and science called economics, (from the Greek, *oikonomos*, for the management of the home), before ecology, (from the Greek, *oikologos*, for the knowledge of the home). We began to manipulate the home before we knew what we were manipulating. I request that economics be a sub-science of ecology.

The prospect of the third millennium has had an incredible effect. It is incredible how humanity is preparing itself for a new millennium and century. I have pages and pages of events, like the 1995 4th World Conference of Women in Beijing, and so on, up to and beyond the year 2000.

There is a reason for my optimism. For the first time humanity is trying. But we are only in the kindergarten of the global age. We have not yet learned to be the managers of our planet. And this now has to take place. I have just attended the Gorbachev meeting on the State of the World in San Francisco, and I have gained a lot of hope. They had the courage to get some of the best world experts to look into the state of the world and then to look into the future, to create a vision of the society that we want in the next millennium...and then do it. They want to implement the population plan, support simple and frugal lives, and get multinational corporations to acquire global consciousness. This gives me enormous hope. We are really doing it. From a pessimistic young man, when I entered the UN immediately after World War II, I have become a very optimistic old man.

Let me give you some very specific recommendations and ideas:
1) Representation of the NGO's (Non Governmental Organisations) at Habitat II Conference in Istanbul.
2) Create a World Association of Eco-Communities to be a NGO-accredited by the UN.
3) Support the UNESCO Planet Society program.
4) I would create a world ecological university here at Findhorn.
5) Hold a meeting or conference of long term evolutionary scientists, because they are now switching to thinking that it will be global consciousness that will be saving humanity, and will install humanity as the most advanced species on this planet.
6) Mobilise any groups that are in favour of simple, frugal living in the developed countries.
7) Ask the UN to hold a conference on garbage, built-in obsolescence, and waste.
8) Ask Gorbachev to create a world commission on the denuclearisation of this planet.
9) Request a world conference for rural development and the stabilisation of the villages.
10) The demilitarisation of this planet — starting with Findhorn asking for the closure of the RAF base next door.
11) Support the World Commission on the Oceans.
12) Look into the errors of transferring Western values and technologies into the developing countries.
13) Celebrate World Environment Day, and other days, that support a global consciousness around nature.

To finish, when you speak of eco-villages, *oikos* —the home, I would develop a whole strategy which would go from the 'eco-self', the management of my own person, to the 'eco-family', the 'eco-school', the 'eco-village', the 'eco-neighbourhood', the 'eco-city', the 'eco-region', the 'eco-nation'; replace NATO with the North Atlantic Community of Nations or NACAM. And finally, to have an 'eco-earth', from the 'eco-self' to the 'eco-universe', to have a total strategy of having our home cleaned of all the nonsense with which it is filled today.

We need to actively practise good public relations, spread the word. Last year I decided to write down an idea that would help bring these changes about every day until the year 2000. These ideas may seem crazy, but then you meet someone who will be very happy to implement them. Out of about 540 ideas so far, about 40 have been implemented. There are still about 1643 days to have ideas. Remember Margaret Mead's saying, it is only a little group of people who can change the world — ideas change the world.

Robert Mueller went to work as a trainee at the UN when it was a fledgling organisation. Since then, he has served as an Under-Secretary for many years. In his retirement he became Chancellor of the UN University for Peace in Costa Rica.

Habitat II
The Second United Nations Conference on Human Settlements will be held in Istanbul, Turkey from 3-14 June 1996. The Global Eco-Village Network will be taking part in the NGO forum, which about 12,000 people are expected to visit. For further information contact the GEN International Secretariat at: Gaia Villages, Skyumvej 101, Snedsted, 7752 Denmark. Tel: +45 9793 6655
Fax: +45 9793 6677
e-mail: gen@gaia.org

Dr. Robert Mueller
UN University for Peace in Costa Rica
PO Box 138
Costa Rica, Central America
Tel +506 249 1072
Fax +506 249 1929

plenary sessions

SAVE THE EARTH   Jonathon Porritt

*Jonathon Porritt has been
an environmental
campaigner, in the UK
and worldwide, for more
than twenty years. He
has worked as the
director for Friends of the
Earth and the leader of
the Green Party in
Britain. He is the co-
founder of Forum for the
Future, a partnership of
independent experts
committed to building a
sustainable way of life.
Jonathon is the author of*
Seeing Green *and* Save
the Earth.

*Jonathon Porritt
Thornbury House
18 High Street
Cheltenham GL50 1DZ*

*Tel +44 (0)1242-262737
Fax +44 (0)1242-262757*

I start today feeling pretty upbeat. What is going on here, and in the Green Movement, is a realisation of our potential; a coming to maturity of ideas and practice, in a way that astonishes people in the Green Movement more than anybody else. And that's what I want to talk about today. Although we're making enormous strides in terms of our ability to reach different audiences and change perceptions, we seem to have a perception of ourselves that is not very different from what it was ten years ago. And in many ways, our ability to play to these audiences now, and to make these ideas work in peoples' lives, is being dramatically hampered by that lack of realisation.

I have been on the advisory council of The Earth Centre for six years. At the start, everybody said: "You have got to be bonkers - it's so big. You can't possibly think that a Green idea is going to get £50 or £100 million." The Earth Centre got it's funding. Why? Because we've got the best ideas about how to bring solutions to people today.

Everybody is talking about community. And I was delighted to hear that you haven't spent a lot of time defining the word community, because that gives me a wonderful opportunity to try to do so. I thought that I would start from the conventional thinking of what is now known as the communitarian movement. I'm going to look at five central tenets of the communitarian movement and how what I call 'eco-communitarianism' is adding to these central tenets.

The first tenet relates to scale. **At long last it seems the concept of human scale has actually emerged as a serious piece of political and sociological understanding.** So what are the eco-communitarians adding to that? Two things. Firstly, the notion of appropriateness of scale; human scale needs to be geared appropriately to the different contexts in which human beings are living and working. We can add an ecological understanding of scale, in terms of the number of human beings, but also in the degree to which those human beings are dependent on the surrounding environment. Secondly, a little bit of precision, of rigour, in the way the word 'community' is used. Because there are a lot of abuses of the word 'community'; like the 'business community'. Call them what you like, but not communities. A community has to be embedded in a place; in a hard edged, physical, tangible, place. That is the essence of what ecologists bring to the debate about community; that it is rooted and embedded, ecologically and culturally.

The second tenet in communitarianism today is the desire to correct the balance between rights and responsibilities. The thesis runs that the attribution of rights has gone too far, and we have not allowed for a proper balancing or weighting of responsibilities to match those rights. And I have to say that I agree with a very large part of this. At the heart of Green politics is an acknowledgement of responsibilities; to the Earth and all it's creatures, and to people of the present and future. But the conservatism of a genuine, ecological, social contract is rather different than that.

Edmund Burke, one of the first and most profound thinking conservatives in modern history, said this: "The social contract exists between those who are living, those who are dead, and those who are yet to be born. Through this contract freedom should not be interpreted as individual libertarianism, but rather that state of things in which liberty is secured only by the equality of restraint." Where is that equality of restraint today? Where, in what postures as conservatism today, do you find anything that is genuinely to do with conservatism? For conservatism as a political movement has been taken over by the insidious virus of neo-liberal individualism. But conservatism features very largely indeed in Green politics. It is part of our politics, and I think we are, foolishly, nervous about articulating that part of our politics.

Thirdly, communitarianism reconfirms the importance of voluntary action, of more independent forms of wealth creation and distribution in the local economy. But this is a very frail form of communitarianism, because it is about is treating the casualties of our failure to make the global economy work in the way that it once did. The global economy can't deliver the goods. It cannot deliver both a permanently, exponentially growing economy and something like full employment, when the only way to become more productive is by getting rid of people.

And I have to say that **long before an ecological collapse, caused by global warming or whatever, our societies will implode, simply because we cannot find a mechanism of giving people access to gainful, meaningful work.** So for Greens, when we talk about the local economy, and about alternative patterns of wealth creation, we are talking about a strategic commitment to a different way of generating wealth. Now you've heard from Guy Dauncey and Robert Gilman, and many others, and it is at long last beginning to dawn on people that this is not a second class, can't-quite-make-it-in-the-real-world type economy. This is actually the economy upon which all our futures depend.

Fourthly, community is seen as being at the heart of post-modernism, as the state was once seen as being at the heart of collectivism. I actually don't know what post-modernism is. But I do know that the language of post-modernism remains narrowly technocratic, narrowly to do with our manipulation and management of society and people. So what does eco-communitarianism add here? It adds the notion of community as a living integrated system; people embedded in a living community. People are beginning to understand that we are intricately connected with other living systems, and that our wellbeing and livelihoods depend on them.

Lastly, communitarianism today has a very powerful strand of ethics. There is a strong sense of there being a breakdown in the moral order. There is a growing horror of the degree to which our economic systems seem to depend on the cultivation of greed and self-interest. However, as articulated by conventional communitarians, there is something disturbingly nostalgic about this looking backward to a golden age that never existed. What do the eco-communitarians add to that? We add a spirituality to the ethical dimension of communitarianism—just being at Findhorn, I don't really need to say anything more about it.

We add to the communitarian mix five crucial ingredients: the notion of community as embedded place; as social contract; as living livelihood; as natural system; and as spirituality. I think that eco-communitarianism is a revolution in waiting; the most astonishing body of ideas, principles and practice that the world has ever seen. Yet we tend to talk to ourselves about it. I'm worried that we don't spend more time on each of these different points talking to those for whom they have a natural sympathy. When we talk about community as embedded place, why do we find it so difficult to communicate that essence to farmers? When we talk about community as social contract, why do we find it so difficult to talk to conventional politicians about what we mean by that? Eco-communitarians have to engage in the political system. If we don't we are simply copping out. We need to talk to anybody who will listen to the growing authority of Green ideas.

So all those people are there waiting to be talked to. But who do we actually end up talking to? We spend an awful lot of time talking to ourselves. We are very nervous about talking to people outside of our charmed little circle. And we tend to fall into five serious traps, five sins:

1) Masturbationism. Safe and quite fun. The great problem with it is that it doesn't go much further than yourself. So the first rule of this new paradigm of eco-communitarianism is don't do it with yourself, do it with someone else. It's more fun, and you may end up giving birth to something new.

2) Escapism. Greens seek refuge in eco-communities because they can't bear the horrors of the unsustainable world in which they live. So the second rule of eco-communitarianism is: Don't opt out, opt in. We can opt in through Local Agenda 21, through engagement in the wider community, or through engagement in political parties. Opting out is a lethal self-indulgence that we can no longer afford.

3) Isolationism. This is linked to the previous sin. By isolationism I mean the idea that because we're doing it that's enough. There is no need to talk

about it. Communication will just happen. Well of course it won't. So don't isolate yourself, communicate.

4) Alternativism. The Green Party loves it's alternativism. It cannot bear the thought that it may have to engage in the mainstream, that one day it might be held to be orthodoxy. And in being attached to our alternativism we tend to marginalise ourselves. So get into the mainstream as fast as you possibly can.

5) Moral Superiority. Part of that moral superiority is that we end up demonising people, people who may only be unable to deal with the challenge that is now laid upon them. Don't demonise, empathise. And if you can't empathise, subvert.

What I have given you is a model for eco-communitarianism in the real world, engaging with people in partnerships to make these ideas and projects have a far bigger currency than they currently have. We all know what the source of our strength is in this movement. We all know what that common core of values is: that love of human kind, that reverence for the Earth, that compassion for people in the world today. We know that. All I can really say to end this conference is go back and walk your talk. And then just watch, and see things change.

SUSTAINING ECO-VILLAGES
Alan Watson Featherstone

"What is the use of a house if you haven't got a tolerable planet to put it on?"
—Henry David Thoreau

What is the use of an eco-village if you haven't got a tolerable planet to put it on?

In looking at eco-villages and sustainable communities, the most important community we need to create sustainability for is the Community of Life. Humanity is one of an estimated 30 million species on Earth, but our actions and impact are now out of all proportion with the continued survival of most of those other species, which all have a part to play in the wellbeing and ongoing evolution of the planet.

Before we can have sustainable human communities, or sustainable development, we must have sustainable ecosystems. The pioneering eco-villages of today are primarily focussing their efforts on minimising their impact on the planet, and thereby reducing humanity's negative impact on the material world, through better use of 'resources' and benign technologies, and this primarily limits any further destruction. However, we do not to the same extent address the damage already done to the planet, and for us to be real role models for a sustainable future, I believe that we need to become active in the healing of the Earth, to be advocates of all life on the planet, and therefore to stand for much more radical changes in our industrial-materialistic culture than we do at present.

Eco-villages have an important role in sustaining the Community of Life. Eco-villages must articulate a philosophy which enables the nonhuman species to continue to live on the planet. By embracing Deep Ecology, they can become "Deep Eco-villages". In the post-industrial era, one of the first tasks awaiting humanity is to assist the healing of the Earth, and for eco-villages to be relevant, we must become active participants in this. The use of renewable energy, appropriate technologies, etc., and the creation of human communities then become part of the larger purpose of being advocates for all life on Earth. Eco-villages should become bioregional focal points for the restoration of ecosystems (so that they become sustainable again), initiating projects to get their bioregion back to health.

What have polar bears known of tropical rainforests, or earthworms known of whales and galaxies? For the first time in evolution, knowledge of all of these things has come together in human minds. It is humanity collectively in our interconnectedness which encompasses this, for it is too vast a knowledge, and too complex, for individuals or groups of individuals to hold. Now, with our modern technology and the ancient wisdom that the Earth is alive, we provide the framework complex enough for the nascent self-consciousness of the living planet to come into expression.

Much of my inspiration and work is now devoted to helping the regeneration of the native Caledonian Forest in the Highlands of Scotland. This has been prompted by my increasing sensitivity to the land here, and I feel the empty glens and hills calling out to me on some inner level for the return of the forest. Acting on this inspiration, my heart has opened to the trees and I feel a tremendous love for them. Although I have known that this is affecting them in some deep, but significant way, I have nonetheless been surprised at some of the results.

One of my regular activities is looking for pine seedlings in areas of former forest, or where the trees are still declining. Frequently, I find a seedling growing in a precise place I've checked before, where I know none existed even a short time ago. This is the case with a photograph I took in October 1990. I noticed a pine seedling growing on top of a heart-shaped burl on a tree. It's extremely unusual for a seedling to grow directly under a mature tree, and when I photographed this tree a year or two before, there was no seedling there. This tree is a particular favourite of mine.

For me the connection between my love and appreciation for this tree and the appearance of the seedling (especially as it's growing on top of *heart-shaped* burl) is of profound importance. It is living confirmation of the Deva messages, that love is the essence of all life and that it has the power to make vegetables, pine seedlings and people grow and blossom into their full potential. Loving the world and all it contains is a powerful and practical spiritual action, and for me is the key to healing the earth and transforming humanity.

Alan Watson Featherstone is the director of Trees for Life at the Findhorn Foundation, Scotland.

Alan Watson Featherstone
Trees for Life
Findhorn Foundation
The Park, Findhorn
Forres,
Moray IV36 0TZ
Scotland

Tel +44 (0) 1309 691292
Fax +44(0) 1309 691155

treesfor life@gn.apc.org

THE GLOBAL ECO-VILLAGE NETWORK
Ross Jackson

To talk about the origins of GEN, the Global Eco-Village Network, we have to go back to 1987 when Hildur and I, and a few friends with a similar vision founded the Gaia Trust with the idea of promoting the transformation to sustainability. We asked ourselves how we could best use the resources we had. Hildur and I had lived in a cohousing for about twenty years, and that was something we thought could be built upon. But we were both very disillusioned by the lack of response to the warning signals that had been sent out almost twenty years earlier by the Meadows Report, and others. The whole society seemed to be in denial. I think Robert Mueller hit the nail on the head when he talked about the systemic flaw in the way we have organised ourselves on the planet. The nation-state basically has sovereignty as its first priority. It really has no global mandate. Whereas the corporations, which have become even more powerful than many nation-states, are operating globally, but they are only operating in their own self interest. What this means is that the only agent for change is civil society.

We became convinced that the eco-villages concept was a key component in any global strategy to manifest the eco-spiritual vision. We know what the problems are; we know what the solutions are and we have all the technology we need to solve the problems. The basic problem is implementation. And realising this got us to understand that what is needed are good examples of what sustainable living really means. We decided that the best way for us to use our funds was to go out and support the people who were actually doing it; the eco-villagers.

At Gaia Trust we developed, not a three legged stool or a four legged stool, but a two legged stool. We came up with what we called the yin-yang solution. We came up with Gaia Technologies and Gaia Villages.

J.T. Ross Jackson, Ph. D., is chairman of Gaia Trust, Denmark. He and wife Hildur lived for twenty years in one of the first co-housing projects in Denmark. His background is in operations research and international finance. He is a naturalised Danish citizen, born in Canada.

*Ross Jackson
Storkevænget 8
2840 Holte*

*Tel +45 4242 5581
Fax +45 4242 5591
ross@gaia.org*

For more information on the Global Eco-Village Network (GEN), see the Workshop and Resource Sections.

One of the major problems with the eco-village concept is jobs. Many people want to live in an eco-village, but don't have a way of supporting themselves. We felt it was very important, that in parallel with the Gaia Villages, we help develop technologies that would be appropriate to place in these villages, to create jobs.

In 1991 we asked Robert and Diane Gilman of The Context Institute to do a survey of existing eco-villages, *The Eco-Village Report*. Then we brought together people from some of the best examples we could find. One of the most important outcomes from that meeting was that people from this group began working together on new projects. We realised that just creating opportunities for networking was in itself a valuable thing to do. We also realised that the eco-villagers' real needs were financial, and far beyond what we could help them with.

(At this point, unexpectedly, a butterfly flew into the Universal Hall and fluttered around Ross.)

Next I met Stephan Wik, who introduced me to what is happening on the Internet. The Internet is moving from being a specialised vehicle to becoming a mainstream way of communicating. This network is expanding at a phenomenal rate and will change the power structure of the world. It's going to bring power into the hands of individuals. Consumers will be able to circumvent the middleman and go straight to the producer. It isn't going to happen immediately, but it is going to happen. We realised this was a very important tool for what we were trying to do. This isn't a substitute for community, but it is an important tool. It is important for a group like this that is very thinly dispersed around the globe. It enables us to build a power base on a very low-cost basis.

Today we have a seed group, but no formal network. Based on the feedback we've received this week, our main goal is to create regional networks. In Denmark, where we organised 15 communities, the parliament is now asking this group to come and comment on legislation. That would never happen to an individual. We're becoming a player. We're beginning to influence decisions. As a group, we have a much better opportunity to fundraise, learn from each others' mistakes, and attract members.

We think the Internet is the best way to encourage the growth of GEN. We have pages up on the Net that show the existing seed group. Soon we will be able to produce resource lists and link specialists from around the world. There will be how-to manuals on, for example, how to formulate articles for an organisation, and how to make an application for funding. There can be special interest groups focusing on business ideas and financing, permaculture, ecological building, and village design. Trade is another goal further down the road. Our hope is to link individual villagers with the producers so they can buy and sell directly with one another. In effect we have the potential of developing an autonomous, alternative economy.

I'd like to say a few words about organisation. Our role at Gaia Trust is to act as a catalyst, to help you do what you're doing. Our feeling is that rather than funding particular projects and villages, in the future we will be primarily funding the infrastructure, that is, communication.

A metaphor which I find describes what is happening on the planet right now is that of metamorphosis, of a caterpillar changing into a butterfly. This is a metaphor that has deep personal meaning for me. Biologically, what happens is that when the caterpillar goes into its cocoon, there begin to appear independent cells that are treated as foreign matter by the caterpillar. Its immune system initially rejects this foreign matter, until gradually some of these independent cells link together and form so-called imaginal disks, a ring-like structure of several cells. The rings become very powerful and the point comes when they can no longer be rejected. They link together and form an indestructible network. And gradually the new network takes over the dying organism. That's what we're doing here. We're establishing the foundation of a new culture. We're going through a metamorphosis.

In closing, I'd like to share a personal experience I had, and this is the first time I've spoken about this publicly, but it seems appropriate in this connection. In 1982, I spent a week with Swami Muktananda at his ashram in India, and I had the most remarkable experience of my life. It's almost impossible to describe it, but I'll do the best I can. What I experienced there was a literal awakening similar, I imagine, to what a butterfly experiences. It was a shift in consciousness that was as great as the difference between sleep and waking. I was somehow being shown a state of consciousness that I think we're all heading for. I think others have experienced the same. For me it was a tremendous personal inspiration to try to integrate the spiritual with the material. I would like to pass this on, because this state is very real. It is going to happen.

Welcome to the Future!

Living Machine Opening   13 October 1996

The opening of the first Living Machine in Europe was presided over by Michael Shaw, of Living Technologies, USA. The opening was attended by members of the water industry, local community members and, of course, the conference delegates. Speakers included: John Todd, the designer of the Living Machine; Lama Yeshe of the Samye Ling Retreat Centre, and Jonathon Porritt. Lama Yeshe blessed the Living Machine with a Tibetan prayer.

In a Living Machine, waste water is pumped to large underground holding tanks that serve as anaerobic reactors where much of the solid matter is digested. The stream then moves through a series of open tanks that each has a unique ecosystem of microorganisms and plants which break down wastes and absorb them as nutrients. At the midpoint suspended solids are collected and recycled to the anaerobic reactors. Finally a set of tanks called ecological fluidised beds filled with local and exotic aquatic plants and animals complete the cycle with final polishing. After that the water is ready for garden reuse or discharge in the local watercourse.

Conference participants and Findhorn community members brought local aquatic plants and animals to place in the open tanks.

"Twenty-five years ago, almost to the day, the ecologist Howard Odum made a radical suggestion: 'Wouldn't it be wonderful if engineers and ecologists got together and turned their collective knowledge back, and tried to understand how nature works; how a mangrove swamp or a lake might work, and to transform that knowledge into living technologies that would serve human beings without destroying the planet.'

"In the past 25 years there have been experiments throughout the world where engineering and ecology have come together, and a new field has been created, called ecological engineering. We have begun to realise that it is possible to reduce the human impact on the natural world by creating the partnership of the natural world and humans in a new way. The facility here represents the first expression of this in this kind of climate in this part of the world. These ideas can be applied throughout the world, with universal principles.

"By the time the sewage reaches the end tank it is extremely high quality water. The organic material has been reduced; the toxic ammonia has been changed into nitrogen gas; any metals present have been sequestered; and most of the pathogens associated with humans will have been destroyed. From here to the end of the room is an extraordinary panoply of life, ranging from microscopic bacteria to higher plants, trees, fishes, and freshwater molluscs. It's all of them working together, supported by the human engineering. It is a living ecology, about to be woken up."

—John Todd

Special Thanks to: Lyle Schnadt, Anna Marriott and the entire building crew, Michael Shaw of Living Technologies, USA; Alec Walker , Patrick Nash, and John Talbott of Living Technologies Ltd.; Simon Thurgood and Angus Marland of Watershed Systems, Edinburgh; The Highlands and Islands Partnership Program, Tom Clarke, Michael Ogden and the entire Findhorn Foundation Community.

ECOLOGICAL BUILDING IN A COLD CLIMATE
Frederica Miller

Frederica Miller is an architect, permaculture designer, and a member of the GAIA-group in Norway. The GAIA-group has pioneered ecological building practices and design in Norway for ten years, focusing on small scale, locally based projects. Frederica recently initiated the JERA project to establish an eco-village near Oslo.

Frederica Miller
Gartnerveien 4
1450 Nesoddtangen
Norway

Tel +47 22561768 or
+47 6691 9861
Fax +47 22561764

Ecological building in cold climatic conditions — in areas with freezing winter conditions, high moisture and wind — requires careful consideration and ingenuity. The workshop discussed some of the details of ecological building through a slide show. It has been said that we know enough about the practicalities of ecological building. Perhaps some people know enough, but certainly too few people do. There is, for example, much confusion about what a 'breathing wall' is.   For Frederica, the sophistication of design relies on the right practice of details, and this applies to many different levels of life.

Frederica believes that the outer world reflects our inner world, and vice versa. The state of the art of ecological building now reflects the fact that we have only just begun to understand how to build ecologically sophisticated homes. We can only imagine how wonderful buildings will be when we've reached a stronger level of understanding of our inner and outer natural worlds.

The building is a shelter, a skin, that is is adapted to the outer realities of climate and place. If it is built badly, you freeze or your building rots. It is also adapted to the inner realities of our own requirements for physical comfort and aesthetic pleasure. Aesthetics being the creation of what is pleasing for all the senses.

This means that the following principles can be included as part of ecological building:
• Buildings must be adapted to the local climate and site, so that they are integrated with the
   landscape and vegetation.
• Local renewable building materials and resources should be used, like straw bale construction.
• The building should breathe, ie. have moisture-transfusive and possibly air-transfusive walls
• Construction systems should be made for reuse.
• Buildings should have a healthy indoor climate with healthy materials and natural ventilation systems.
• There should be a reduction of household and sewage waste, with recycling of wastes on site.
• User-friendly technology should be promoted.

For the last forty years we have been building our homes with plastic membranes on the inside. This is a wonderful picture of how desperate we are to distance ourselves from the natural world. Breathing walls were commonly used until forty years ago. They are moisture-transfusive, allowing the movement of moisture from the inside out. They can also be air-transfusive, allowing air to move through the wall fabric. (This however, is new and should be regarded as experimental for the time being.)

When we allow moisture transfusion the benefits are:
• Moisture carries pollution particles with it from the inside out, and
• Osmosis of gases can occur, ie when there is more carbon dioxide inside (which there usually will be) than oxygen outside, the gasses will diffuse through a permeable wall construction, giving the breathing effect.

In practice a vapour barrier is needed on the inside which is five times tighter than the outside wind protection layer. This is an old carpenter's rule of thumb, and has been used in Nordic countries for at least a hundred years. It is quite safe even in coastal climates like Scotland, as seen in the Bag End houses at Findhorn.

An air-open construction uses the principle of dynamic insulation. Here fresh cool air is drawn in with the help of an lower pressure inside through the outer insulation layer, usually a ceiling. The heat loss which is on the way out is then drawn in, giving slightly prewarmed fresh air, and energy savings due to reduced heat loss.

ECO-VILLAGES TO ECO-CITIES: REBUILDING FROM THE GRASSROOTS UP

Richard Register

Richard believes we have three bodies: the living one given at birth; the biosphere, now commonly called Gaia; and a third that few recognise — our built environment, our physical community. This third body is the only one we are free to shape in any major way. Yet we have made it an unhealthy, wildly destructive mess. Richard is convinced we need to re-build our entire civilisation from its foundations up.

A healthy community body or anatomy is based on human measure. It's based on our animal body's dimensions, speeds and requirements for shelter and sustenance (physically, socially and spiritually). Our villages and cities need to be designed for pedestrians, with walkable downtowns and walkable neighbourhoods.

In addition to good organisation that encourages "access by proximity, not transportation," we must also consider population, levels of consumption and specific technologies as equally essential ingredients of a healthy future world. As Paul Ehrlich points out:

Impact on the Planet = Population x Affluence x Technology

The form and arrangement of the whole community, its land-use/infrastructure is also important. Richard calls this the community's "landustructure", (pronounced "land-you-structure"). The landustructure needs to be compact, diverse in its uses, permeated with and immediately adjacent to local biodiversity, and conserve land and energy. It needs to be as durable as possible, support thorough recycling and eventually *be* recyclable or reusable itself. That's it! But the key is in the details.

Richard showed slides of examples of community design and activist projects around the world that attempt to transform cities and villages into eco-cities and eco-villages. He focused primarily on his home town, Berkeley, California, where he showed solar greenhouses made possible by the community's own work in passing new energy ordinances, the uncovering of several creeks and "planter strips" for gardens at low income housing sites.

Eco-city zoning maps are a tool that can be used to guide the transformation of cities toward walkable centres over the next few decades. They enable consolidation of both cities and villages around centres , while opening up nature and agriculture. It's all done with laws, zoning, ordinances, tax and services incentives — and disincentives. It's a very big bag of the usual development schemes, but this time designed with eco-cities and eco-villages in mind.

If rural and urban eco-villagers add traditional village form to their gardening, appropriate technology, healthy building materials and cooperative ways, they will literally, physically, bring all the pieces together. This would mean, for example, that Findhorn should not scatter small, separated buildings across its newly acquired five acres, but instead should define a centre in the Park, a streetscape and perhaps a tiny town square, while constructing new buildings that are three, four, maybe in some cases, five stories high!!! Richard's vision of Findhorn also includes building tall solar greenhouses and using traditional design themes with materials from the area.

What could be magic in this is the fact that both the village and city need to be transformed toward this more compact, pedestrian and far more diverse anatomy, or landustructure. **If clusters of buildings as attractive and well executed as Findhorn's Universal Hall and Cluny Hill College are created and assembled in relatively traditional street-defining patterns, the eco-village movement could create a highly contagious seed to transform not only villages around the world, but cities too.** For Richard, the best legacy of this conference would be to do just this.

*Richard Register is a California-based activist and long-time promoter of urban sustainability. He is president and founder of Ecocity Builders Inc., and editor of the **Ecocity Builder** newsletter. Richard was the founder of Urban Ecology, Inc., the convener of the First Ecocity Conference in Berkeley in 1990, and is working on a book called **Ecocities**.*

Richard Register
Ecocity Builders
5427 Telegraph
Avenue W2
Oakland,
California 94 609
USA

Tel +1 1510 649 1817
Fax +1 1510 699 1817

workshops

ECO-VILLAGES IN THE URBAN CONTEXT
Dirk Bolt

Dirk Bolt is a consultant and professor of Information for Urban Planning and Management at the International Institute for Aerospace Survey and Earth Sciences (ITC). He has developed an ecological design approach to urban planning based on extensive experience in both the developing world and Western society. ITC,PO Box 6, 7500 AA Enschede, The Netherlands.

Dirk Bolt
Burg.E.Beigsmalaan 16
Enschede
The Netherlands

Tel +31 53 4326343
Fax +31 53 4326343

Urbanisation is changing the face of the earth and the future of humankind. **The concept of eco-villages has an important message for the necessary new urban policies, but there can be no new urban policies without new urban strategies.**

In urban planning and management, spatial plans are a key strategy. There is need of an urban spatial strategy that can help implement policies towards a more sustainable and humane urban future. In the spatial concept described below, cities consist not of rings of growth but of a cluster of urban communities. The number is flexible, but they are always grouped to form a circuit. A way of visualising the concept is to imagine the circuit as a necklace in which the beads represent urban communities.

The urban communities do not exceed one kilometre in radius, making it possible to reach public transport stops on foot in less than ten minutes. In the urban communities, all houses, all buildings connect to footpaths. In turn, these connect to a radial system of preferred pedestrian routes. These 'footstreets' lead to the centre of the urban community. The radial emphasis promotes a very high pedestrian concentration in the centre.

The pedestrian system is supplemented by a bicycle system providing access from each house to the centre, and from community centre to community centre. Whereas the human scale of the pedestrian system insures equity in physical access to the centre of the community and to the activities and goods which are located there, access to having choice is provided by the centre-to-centre bicycle routes, and by centre-to-centre public transport.

The urban communities are served by a hierarchy of public transport systems. The first level system is a mechanical extension of the pedestrian system, a horizontal 'lift', linking the centres of the urban communities. The morphology of the system is critical: the system forms a circuit, thus providing equity in access to all centres (either by bus, tram or a fully automated light rail train). This promotes dispersal of workplaces, services and facilities. The second level system has circuit-like characteristics. It connects the cluster-city to other cluster-cities, forming still larger cities. The third level circuits provide linkages between these large cities and other urban constellations in the region.

The main feature of the road system of a typical cluster of urban communities is the inner ring road, which provides equity in access to all communities. As in the case of the public transport circuit, the ring road ensures equity in access to all urban communities. Each of the urban communities is accessed from a horseshoe-shaped outer boundary road, which connects to the inner ring road at the rounded end of the horseshoe. From the boundary road, spur roads provide access to all houses and buildings, without violating the pedestrian domain formed by the system of radial footstreets.

The effect of such a spatial strategy for urban traffic is that traffic origins and destinations are dispersed rather than centralised, hence each urban community has a comparable share of all land uses (i.e., social and economic activities).   In each urban community, there are two kinds of areas where people work: work areas that are compatible with residential land uses, and those that are not, due to noise,etc.. The compatible land uses are arranged along the footstreets. This means that the footstreets are lined with a range of activities (e.g., shops, which increase in specialisation and/or size as they are located nearer to the centre). The non-compatible work quarters of two adjacent urban communities may be arranged next to each other, so as to facilitate interchange between the work areas and thus promoting specialisation, which is a condition of development.

The high concentration of pedestrians in the centre, the location in the centre of the public transport stops and the proximity (one kilometre) of the centres to the inner ring road makes these the natural places for higher density developments of both residential and non-residential land uses. The concentration reduces as one walks from the central square to the periphery of the urban community. There, densities are low. As densities are closely associated with lifestyles, the wide range densities in each urban community implies a range of lifestyles, thus promoting wider opportunity for social access and interaction. The densities are also variable over time. **Rather than spreading over the land at a fixed density (which is what the suburb does), the extent of land-take is limited to one kilometre radius but densities within the urban communities are 'open ended'.**

The spatial strategy promotes the development of a new and more responsible urban technology. For instance, the footstreets can be covered by canopies or roofs. Not only would these provide shelter (thus making it more attractive to use the public transport system), the overhead construction could also function as a platform for duct service carriers such as fibre optics (both for signals and light) and services (like gas and water). In colder climates, water pipes are isolated against frost, thus avoiding the waste of potable water through freezing of pipes and through leakages, which waste as much as 70% of potable water in some cities. The concept of fully accessible, extendible and amendable urban services would promote the introduction of innovative technologies, such as electronic networking and pneumatic systems for the removal of waste to local or adjacent industrial areas, where wasted resources, including energy, could be recycled.

As part of the strategy, energy systems are built from the bottom up, not from the top down. Every house, every (foot)street and every urban community contributes to the energy supply (e.g., by solar panels framing the roofs of the covered footstreets). At the city level, the communities are interlined for mutual support in meeting peaks in energy demand. Only if the cluster as a whole is unable to meet the demand is the supply 'topped up' by a central facility. This strategy leads to a much more autonomous situation, in case of emergency the urban communities have a built-in capability to survive.

In a strategy of improved urban self-reliance, space is needed to raise energy (e.g. by windmills) and to catch and/or store vital resources (e.g. water). Some forms of energy may be dangerous (e.g. natural gas). These, and other vital functions such as communications (e.g., a television tower) or air travel (e.g. vertical take off and landing for aircraft) can only be accommodated if there is space, which is most effective if it is located centrally in relation to the urban communities which are served by the facilities. This space would be available in the form of the central open space within the inner ring road, which can be seen as a spatial contingency allowance. Until the communal needs or uses of the open space are defined, they will be part of the landscape and system of open spaces, discussed next.

In the spatial strategy, energy conservation starts with the landscape. Cold winds are deflected by shelter belts of trees. Parts of the woods are 'working' parks, providing timber, firewood and mulch for the communities. Through such a system of nature corridors, the ancient partnership between man and forest may be returned to the experience of the urban dweller. Inside the urban communities also, trees protect groups of houses from prevailing winds. Trees planted on the sunny side of houses and footstreets are deciduous; cool in summer, sun-warm in winter.

In each of the urban communities, trees and open space are within the reach of the pedestrian. Landscape is not further than a few minutes walk away, often it can be glimpsed from the town centre, which is linked by an urban park (via the open end of the horseshoe-shaped boundary road) to the open space that surrounds the urban community. The open space elaborates the 'useful landscape' theme established by the planting of trees. The wooded areas are interspersed with permaculture plots, market gardens, nurseries, paddocks for ponies and 'pick-your-own' farms. This quilt pattern of 'touchable' land uses the open space contrasts with the larger scale of the agricultural land, or perhaps wilderness areas, beyond. Thus, each urban community is set in its own sphere of sustenance, which may be perceived as miniaturisation of the island named earth. In these environs, in each urban eco-system, a range of environmental experiences lies within the urban child's un-motorized reach, providing ground for understanding and hope.

CREATING COHOUSING: ECO-OPPORTUNITIES AND ECONOMIC CONSTRAINTS   Chris Hanson

Chris Hanson is a full-time cohousing community development consultant with special skills in group process and consensus, land acquisitions, feasibility analysis, design process, development process and financial planning.
He is currently writing Creating Cohousing: Making Your Dreams Come True.

Christopher Hanson
16580 78A Ave
Surrey, B.C.
Y35 7V3
Canada

Tel +1 604 574 1545
Fax +1 604 574 1989

Cohousing started in Denmark in the early seventies when dual income professionals were searching for better child care and a safer neighbourhood. It has matured into an intergenerational mix of family types, attractive to young families, single parents , as well as retired couples and singles. Nearly 200 projects have been completed in Denmark since 1972. More than 20 have been built in North America since 1991, and more than 150 groups are meeting regularly trying to make their projects happen.

Due to limited government support in North America, the early projects have tended to be market rate housing rather than subsidised or low income. However, in Denmark much of the cohousing that is currently being developed is government sponsored rental or cost controlled affordable ownership.

In North America, Chris has observed that cohousing communities are working hard to balance the needs of each individual for both privacy and community: Providing for opportunities to interact with their neighbours while maintaining distinct personal space for retreat from community.

Cohousing is a synthesis of several of the best features of multi-family housing, limited in size to a range of 12 to 40 units. It is designed and often developed by the residents who will live there. Each home is self-sufficient, with a private living, dining, and kitchen areas. Unlike housing built by a developer, a single cohousing community may have many unit types, ranging from studios to four or five bedrooms. Parking is segregated to the edge of the community, away from the private dwellings. Pedestrian circulation is designed to encourage interaction with neighbours. Smaller, more efficient private units allow for a larger "common house" typically programmed to include community oriented spaces, such as food preparation and dining facilities.

Chris has also observed that cohousing communities make the environment a high priority in their development decision making: Learning about the environmental impacts of the development and construction process and choosing to spend more of their resources on environmentally appropriate land, materials and construction methods.

Cost is always the big factor when considering what you can do to be more environmentally appropriate in the development of your community. It takes a substantial level of commitment to accomplish your environmental goals. An individual often feels overwhelmed by the magnitude of the environmental problem and may give in to the contractor's constant harangue about saving money. As a community you can make your decisions about what's important and stand by them, together.

Possibly the largest single environmental decision you will make as a community is your selection of a site. Most of us dream of a pastoral setting, away from the hubbub of the city. But we also want civilisation. You need to consider the true behaviour of the members of your group. Who will be commuting? How far will the kids have to go to school? And what environmental impact will you have as a community in the short term, as well as the long term? The decision between a rural or urban location is a difficult one. Before you choose your site, consider your options carefully. Consider the small town, or the urban village within the city where you live. Do you want to pay the environmental and social price of moving out into the country? Is it your right or your responsibility?

Finally, cohousing groups are working to create communities of diversity: Intentionally attracting people of varying ages, financial and ethnic backgrounds. This includes providing for handicap accessibility, as well as a variety of housing types to meet the wide range of human housing needs and capacities. As individuals we have experience with the creative process. However, we have only just begun to successfully create as communities of individuals working together, co-creating. The cohousing process in North America has been a process of communities of people learning to create together, taking responsibility as a community for a new physical world in which they want to live.

STRAWBALE CONSTRUCTION
David Eisenberg

During three workshop sessions during the week of the conference, David and the workshop participants erected the walls of the first known straw bale structure in Scotland: a loadbearing garden shed measuring 8.2 x 4.4 meters, built with locally grown two string barley straw bales. The bales sit on a concrete stem wall and the building has a concrete foundation. Plywood and 2" x 6" box beam roof bearing assemblies were constructed for each long wall and 2" x 4" roof trusses were also constructed on site.

The garden shed is a loadbearing structure that uses cables to tie the roof to the foundation. Pipe sleeves are embedded through the stem walls about every six feet, to allow the cables to pass under the bale walls and run up over the roof bearing assembly. Short rebar (reinforcing steel) stubs were inserted in the concrete along the centre line of the concrete foundation, to impale the first course of bales and hold them in place.

Each of the three workshop sessions began with an introductory slide show and short question and answer session before going out to the site to work on the building. The hands-on work included learning to retie and make custom sized bales, stacking bales and pinning the bales together with bamboo. The group also discussed bale quality, waterproofing for the bottom of the walls, options for doors and windows, roof plate construction, and a little bit about post and beam versus loadbearing design.

Some participants questioned the appropriateness of building with bales in a wet climate, such as Scotland. **Because straw and wood are very similar in chemical make-up, the same issues must be dealt with in designing and building straw bale structures, as well as wood structures.** The key is to try to keep moisture from entering the walls, and ensuring that what moisture does enter is not trapped. Bale walls which are poorly designed and constructed will be prone to the same type of decay as wood structures, though the process may occur somewhat faster with straw. Water problems in walls are often the result of moisture coming from inside the dwelling and migrating out into the walls, rather than coming from the outside in. As far as energy efficiency is concerned, typical straw bale walls have far greater insulation value than typical wood frame walls.

By the end of the first workshop the group had two courses of bales laid and some custom bales made. After the second workshop, rough window frames were built and installed as the walls went up and the bales at the window openings were bevelled. In the third workshop the last of the custom bale areas of the walls (bevels and a few special size bales) were finished and the roof bearing assemblies were put up on the walls and pinned to the bales.

In the days following the workshop sessions a metal roof was put up. A plaster finish will be put on the exterior walls in the Spring.

David would like to thank Nicole Edmonds, Philip Stewart and Stuart Voder for their help in planning and completing Findhorn's straw bale garden shed.

David Eisenberg is President of the Development Centre for AppropriateTechnology (DCAT) in Tucson, Arizona USA. His building career has progressed from very expensive, resource-intensive buildings, to more sustainable building systems like rammed earth, adobe and straw bale. He heads the Bale Research Advisory Network (BRAN) and has been involved with research, testing and building code issues related to straw bale construction. His current work includes writing about, and developing an international conference on Sustainability and the Building Codes.
He is the co-author of The Straw Bale House.

David Eisenberg
P.O. Box 41144
Tucson AZ 85717
USA

Tel +1 520 326 1418

strawnet@aol.com

workshops

69

MAKING SCHOOL GROUNDS SUSTAINABLE
or THE SCHOOL FOREST LANDSCAPE
Michael Littlewood

Michael Littlewood is an international consultant in sustainable landscape design. He lived and worked in New Zealand for 14 years, holding senior posts in local government and architectural practises. Upon returning to England in 1977 he has focused on landscape architecture and design, authoring two books, publishing numerous articles, and teaching extensively.

Michael Littlewood
Troutwells
Higher Hayne
Roadwater, Somerset
Watchet, TA 23 0RN
UK

Tel +44 (0) 1984 6441330
Fax +44 (0) 1984 6441330

If our children are to have the skills needed to address the environmental problems they will be faced with, we need to be educating them now; not just by incorporating different approaches in the curriculum, but also transforming the school environment to become an education in itself. The school buildings and grounds could provide experiential education—hands on experience in working with nature to provide a greener and more productive environment. If children learn by experience how to utilise solar energy, collect and use rainwater, and plant and harvest their own food, they will take these skills out of school and into the community.

Michael Littlewood is a consultant in sustainable garden and landscape design who sees the potential of schools and their grounds going to waste. **Many schools have not realised the full potential of their 'estates' as an educational and community resource.** Some have simply put in a green strip or wildlife area in a corner. Others have instigated a full environmental audit and phased implementation programme, but even here the full potential for the use of all the buildings and land has not been fully appreciated.

As well as the school becoming a focal point for the local community, school grounds offer the opportunity of providing a neighbourhood ecological park. This is especially pertinent where open space is at a premium, and where the local authority has provided few opportunities for relaxation, contemplation and contact with nature in attractive and nourishing environments. Yet, creating attractive surroundings is only part of the picture. Functional and ethical landscapes which are the basis of Permaculture can also be created.

Rain water can be collected from roofs to create retention/detention ponds which could also be used for irrigation, wildlife habitats, education, and even as 'fire ponds.' Grey water can be recycled through a series of filter beds and 'flow forms' to the ponds/pools/lakes. Solid wastes can be composted and returned to fertilise new woodlands. The Camphill School in Gloucester, UK, recycles its sewage through reed beds.

Trees can be planted not just to enhance, but so that they actively reduce wind velocity and save energy; evergreen climbers used to reduce building heat loss as well as create wildlife habitats. Fruit trees and bushes can be used to produce food for the children even in restricted spaces, where espaliers, cordons, etc. are possible. Useful plants such as herbs, dried flowers, dye plants and vegetables can be incorporated an methods such as companion planting and organic gardening can be demonstrated. This mixed planting or 'plant stocking' could then become the school "Forest Garden"—a whole edible ecosystem modelled on a natural woodland.

If we are serious about conserving natural resources we can turn to third world technology to achieve economic energy saving in school buildings. We can do this by installing cheap solar, wind or hydro systems, and where there is sufficient local land, trees can be used for biomass or fuel.

The School Forest Garden can be used to allow children to rediscover the delights of fresh fruit and vegetables and to demonstrate to all members of the community, particularly children, how the sensitive management of plants, animals, land and buildings can create a life supporting system that neither destroys nor pollutes the planet.

DESIGNING SUSTAINABLE LANDSCAPES FOR HUMAN SETTLEMENTS
Wes Groesbeck and Jan Striefel

Landscapes are reflections of our attitude toward the natural environment. Human impacted landscapes that are not treated respectfully result in erosion, loss of habitat, unnecessary cost and a loss of personal and spiritual connection to the land. There are ways of living and working within natural systems that are regionally responsive. Native plants and recycled materials can be used in parks, public plazas and highway corridors to establish a sense of place and connection between people and the landscape. The natural and built environment can be blended by using native and adapted plant materials which are suited to the climate and location, requiring little or no irrigation. Recycled brick, wood, and concrete as new paving, can be used as places for people to sit and sculptural elements.

In this workshop, Jan and Wes focused on the basic design tools that can be used to enhance water and energy efficiency, as well as the cost benefits of sustainable management of the landscape. In discussing water efficiency, Wes described the steps he took in his own yard in Salt Lake City, Utah,USA. These included: killing the lawn and replacing it with drought-tolerant vegetation suitable to his site; constructing hardscapes of porous materials to allow water to seep slowly into the landscape instead of running down the gutter; covering the landscape with a least five inches of mulch to retain soil moisture; installing recycled barrels to harvest snow melt and rainwater from house and garage roofs for irrigation; establishing a graywater system to water the landscape and installing water efficient toilets, showers and faucets inside his house.

In the US, where 5% of the world's population is currently using approximately 23% of the world's energy resources, energy-efficient landscapes are particularly important. The basic landscape tools that can be used to control the elements that define climate and the factors affecting human comfort include considering the topography, cold air drainage and albedo. The topography of the land, or the degree to which is is hilly or flat, effects the microclimate, water drainage patterns, soil depth and character. The steepness of slopes affects both water runoff and soil stability, but in terms of energy efficiency, it mostly influences cold air drainage. Cold air is heavier than warm air, and tends to flow from convex hills into concave valleys. The most frost-free sites are usually on the upper mid-slopes of valleys. They are warmer, day and night, than either valley floor or ridge. These areas are known as the thermal belt and have long been used for siting villages and favoured growing areas. Albedo, or the ability of a surface to reflect incoming solar radiation is another important design consideration. Landscapes consist of many surfaces, including building roofs and walls, streets, parking lots, and school yards. Each of these surfaces either absorbs or reflects a significant portion of the sunlight falling on it. Modifying the albedo of a building or surrounding landscape can significantly lower or raise the heat build-up from sunlight and reduce the amount of energy needed for heating and cooling.

The benefits of sustainable landscaping are aesthetic as well as energy and cost conserving. Jan showed that native landscaping using, for example, buffalo grass seeding instead of conventional blue grass seeding, can save as much as 30% on the installation costs and up to 80% on maintenance costs.

The workshop group put these basic design tools to use by evaluating the landscape of Bag End, a cluster of six houses in the Findhorn Foundation Park. Their suggestions included using plantings as protection from winds, placing the evergreen trees so that they don't inhibit sun penetration, adding edible landscape elements to the design, establishing a communal herb garden, and installing a fire protection system.

Wes and Jan are co-authors of The Resource Guide to Sustainable Landscapes and Gardens. *Wes' Utah based consulting firm, Environmental Resources Inc., provides in-depth assessment for businesses and residences in energy efficiency, health and safety concerns. He has taught sustainable living practices at the University of Utah and a local elementary school. Jan's landscape architecture and urban design business, Landmark Design, Inc., manages and designs a broad range of sustainable landscape projects. One of her greatest pleasures is spending a day 'playing' in her naturescaped garden.*

Wes Groesbeck
2041 East Hollywood
Avenue
Salt Lake City ,
UT 84108-3148
USA
Tel +1 801 485 0280
Fax +1 801 485 0280

Jan Striefel
153 West Pierpont Avenue
Salt Lake City, UT 84101
USA
Tel +1 801 363 3500
Fax +1 801 363 3543

workshops

*Babs Rentjes trained as
an architect and became
head of the municipal
services for the preserva-
tion of monumental
buildings in Kampen
and Amsterdam, the
Netherlands, before
reevaluating her
aspirations and setting
up her own business.
She works for national
and local planners,
facilitating workshops,
brainstorm sessions and
visualisations. She is
particularly smitten
with social pioneering
work that guides
inhabitants to create
and enrich their living
environment—and
would love to be a
midwife to similar
processes in her own
neighbourhood.*

*Fransje de Waard has a
degree in tropical
forestry and environ-
mental planning and
did agroforestry work in
Kenya and Andalucia
before discovering
permaculture. Tired of
being hard up, she has
created De Waard
Edible Landscapes,
distributes
permaculture books,
organises design courses
and workshops, and is
now busy writing the
first thorough Dutch
book on permaculture.*

*For more information on
GAP-Ecoteams, see
Marilyn Mehlmann's
GAP workshop.*

*Fransje de Waard
Box 93108
1090 BC Amsterdam
Tel +31 2996 84227
fransje@xs4all.nl*

*Babs Rentjes,
Volkerakstraat 24 II
1078 XS Amsterdam
Tel +31 20 6751733
Fax +31 20 6720066*

AWAKENING THE DEADLY BORED: ACTIVISM FOR NEIGHBOURHOOD ABUNDANCE

Babs Rentjes and Fransje de Waard

Babs Rentjes lives in the River Neighbourhood in south Amsterdam. Rivers tend to flow, but things in this neighbourhood aren't exactly dynamic. Apart from the usual car and parking pains there are no obvious problems in this area. The problem lies beneath the surface: there is no sense of community. The place is pretty much dead.

Without the drug and crime problems of other areas, the River Neighbourhood isn't singled out for assistance by the local government. Yet boredom, too, is a serious problem that shouldn't be overlooked. Among the workshop participants it was clear that boredom is a real issue in their neighbourhoods; either their own boredom, their frustration to activate others around them, or their concerns over boredom and apathy among youth. Babs and Fransje used the workshop as an opportunity to get suggestions for the River Neighbourhood and to allow participants to brainstorm on ways to 'awaken' their own neighbourhoods.

The River Neighbourhood is like many others. There are cars everywhere, little or no room for kids to play and tiny, private backyards with fences that block most of the sunlight. There is an impressive park nearby, the core of which is an old, medicinal herb garden. The future of the garden is in question, however, because the man who maintains it has back problems and the municipality has no financial means to employ another gardener. The future of the park is also uncertain because a metro train has been planned that would run straight through it. How can this neighbourhood be awakened to become a living community with a diversity of public spaces?

During the workshop, the participants took five minutes to write down their thoughts on boredom and lack of community, imagining themselves as inhabitants of the area. Next, they wrote down what they would do about it and how they would start; asking themselves what they would really want to put into it, and what would light their own fire. Then, miraculously, they were told, it turns out that others on their same street were asking themselves the same questions. The participants then joined into five groups, each representing an actual street in the River Neighbourhood and brainstormed further. After this, a neighbourhood meeting was called where the different streets presented their ideas.

One person thought he would start by simply having his afternoon tea out on the sidewalk, hoping to get in touch with his neighbours. One group did a design for their street, blocking off some of the traffic and parking, to create a sitting space with benches. Others planned to start an afternoon cafe. Another participant offered to share his printing skills with youth in the area so that a neighbourhood newspaper could be started. Maintaining the herb garden and forming a womens' group were also suggested.

Participants were clearly inspired by each other, and said so in the feedback round. Many realised their skills, interests and passions. **The presentation of a real situation which was not their own gave them the freedom to be creative and bold, and think without the perceived limitations of their own situations.**

The results were new ideas, new courage and new inspiration for the participants, and for Babs and Fransje. The River Neighbourhood as it is today continues to challenge them. They like to think that over time more connections will be developed between local urban groups, GAP-Ecoteam programmes and Local Agendas. They think of their efforts as 'ABUN-dance': Activism for Bored Urban Neighbourhoods - dance.

COMMUNITY BUILDING WITH PERMACULTURE
Maddy Harland

There is no doubt that much of permaculture is about developing ways of gardening, farming and building which work with Nature, not against it, and are harmonious rather than destructive. But permaculture is more than a system of garden, house or farm design, it is a holistic approach to creating human settlements which enriches all communities, not just the humans!

To illustrate my point I have a simple story of transformation. Back in 1989, Tim Harland saw a film "In Grave Danger of Falling Food" in which Bill Mollison explained the permaculture concept. The effect was instant and Tim decided that permaculture was exactly what he had been looking for—a coherent strategy for conservation, increased personal sufficiency and community empowerment.

He began by persuading me, his wife, and a group of friends to help him design and plant a permaculture garden. Their first task was to sow a wildflower meadow on a third of an acre of an over-ploughed, barren field. They then planted over sixty mixed fruit and nut trees. Slowly, ecological diversity returned. Insects were attracted by the fragrant and beautiful wildflowers, birds came to perch on the thin trees and slugs and snails came, attracted by our mulched beds in the vegetable plot!

We were mindful of Bill Mollison's comment that an excess of slugs is an absences of ducks, so the next step was to introduce ducks and chickens to feed on the pests and supply us with protein. They also supplied us with a form of currency — eggs — to share with our friends who helped us. Extending this practise of exchange, our friends also helped us to set up a LETS group (Local Exchange Trading Scheme), and enthusiasm for the garden and the ideas behind permaculture spawned a local permaculture group.

Throughout this time of planting, building chicken runs, scavenging materials and setting up local networks, we were also developing *Permaculture Magazine* — again, Tim's brainchild — from its small and fragile base of 600 readers to a self-sufficient publication which is read by thousands. *Permaculture Magazine* was always intended to be an 'outreach' project, to spread the ideas and inspiration, joys and challenges of practising permaculture in colder climates. Again, this was strongly supported by our growing local community of friends, some of whom work on the Magazine and others who support it in spirit. This support has enabled us to publish a source of networking contacts and practical information for permaculture enthusiasts all over the world.

And what of today? Permaculture still continues to transform our lives. The original garden is gradually becoming more abundant and is a home for increasing insects, birds and other animals as well as for edible plants, most of which are perennial. We are still trading LETS enthusiastically, swapping plants, sharing resources and planning to retrofit our houses ecologically. We are also involved in a local project to transform a former British naval communications base to a Centre of Sustainability, demonstrating new technology, permaculture, ecological building and providing an educational resource for the community.

Just a few years ago, hardly anyone had heard of permaculture and we sometimes felt that our task of practising it ourselves and spreading the word was fairly insurmountable Today we are deeply encouraged by the interest and enthusiasm we find not only in our local community, but farther afield in local government, conservation organisations, and of course internationally from the readers of *Permcaulture Magazine*. And when we pause to reflect on what permaculture has brought us, it is not only the great pleasure of watching natural diversity return to our site, or a thriving LETScheme in the community, it is a deep reconnection with the earth which not only feeds our bodies but our souls, and allows us to share this abundance with others.

Written by Maddy Harland. Maddy is the editor of Permaculture Magazine— Ecological Solutions for Everyday Living, *a publication dedicated to practical information on temperate permculture. She is also a regular guest editor for* Planetary Connections *as well as a founding director and Vice Chair of the Earth Works Trust Sustainability Centre's management board. Maddy has published two books, numerous articles and has been giving interactive workshops for many years.*

For a free copy of the Magazine and a catalogue of over 80 useful titles, see the Resource Section.

Maddy Harland
Permaculture Publications
Hyden House LTD.
Little Hyden Lane
Clanfield
Hants PO8 ORU
UK

Tel +44 (0)1705 596500
Fax +44 (0)1705 595834

permaculture@gn.apc.org

workshops

DEVELOPING SUSTAINABLE COMMUNITIES
Jane Hera

Jane Hera has worked in the permaculture field since 1990. She co-founded Designed Visions which works in many fields, including design work for gardens and farms, and the Sustainable Development Initiative. She has assisted the start up of two LETS systems; one local, in Oxford and one international, the Permaculture Exchange.

For more information on permaculture, see the Resources section.

Jane Hera
8 Helen Road
Oxford
OX2ODE
UK

Tel +44 (0)1865 721922
Fax +44 (0)1865 244412

heraford@gn.apc.org

It often happens that when design professionals ask members of a community for their comments and approval on a project, the community members find themselves at a loss for words. Dense information, the smartness of the presentation, time pressure and the observers' lack of familiarity with organised assessment procedures can make it difficult to comment on a project, not to mention approve it. Knowing this, the team at Designed Visions tries to involve community members in every stage of the design process.

The workshop covered two of Designed Visions' projects, the Hemyock Village Design Festival and Springfields Community Gardens. In both projects the client who is paying the fee, the local government, is different from the client who will use and develop the design, the local community. In both cases the processes used in developing the design were chosen to encourage connection with the local community.

The Village Design Festival came a year and a half after the Designed Visions team began working in the Blackdown Hills, an area of outstanding natural beauty in Devon. Here, the Sustainable Development Initiative has been exploring more sustainable agricultural practises amongst farmers and smallholders as well as researching the impact of sustainable development on a large, existing village. A reference group of local people had been meeting during this time for presentations, slide shows and discussions around the principles and practices of Permaculture.

The Design Festival was the opportunity to extend this information to a wider community and took place over three days on the village green at Hemyock. The design of the components ensured that children were made welcome and could interact with several of the displays, particularly those concerning wind and solar energy. Other exhibits included an architectural model of a futuristic solar village and a 1:500 scale map of Hemyock and the surrounding area, presented as a 'Planning for Real' device. This map enabled local people to discuss the future development of Hemyock. The discussions were especially aided by the presence of a number of past and present Councillors for the area. And of course, the Designed Visions team was on hand to talk to people during the festival.

Even though there was a great deal of information available, in the form of displays and leaflets, many visitors said that the personal contact was the most important part for them. The outdoor cafe served drinks and snacks so that people could sit in the sun and browse through the books and magazines at their leisure. The sociable quality of the event was an important design feature.

The Springfield project, on the Holmewood Estate in Bradford, was initiated by the local community. All design work was actively specified and modified at every phase by community members and methods of working were chosen which allowed easy participation. The simple surveying method of observing water levels, for example, enabled local children to become involved in the work, an area normally reserved for professionals in yellow hats. Design proposals were presented in draft form using a 3D model with a walk through storyline. Many significant observations and design modifications arose from this process.

The workshop also described classic permaculture methods, such as swales (channels on contour used to collect runoff water and enable it to move through the soil) and their adaptation to the particular conditions existing at Springfields.

There is high unemployment and often low self esteem amongst many residents of the adjoining Holmewood estate and the Springfields project has gone some way to alleviating these problems. Several local people have become involved as volunteers. The project is evolving to meet the needs and interests of those local people who are becoming involved, with the intention that they will take over the development and operation of Springfields in the future.

workshops

GLOBAL ACTION PLAN FOR THE EARTH
Marilyn Mehlmann

It is nothing new to say that our environment faces big problems. Yet people are often overwhelmed by these problems and end up feeling they can't be effective in solving them. The Global Action Plan for the Earth (GAP) helps people turn their desire to do the right thing into action. GAP is a strategic, result-oriented NGO initiative. Fully realised, the Global Action Plan will substantially contribute to the reversal of high resource consumption and pollution.

GAP's goal is to empower a critical mass of citizens to permanently redesign their lifestyles. When this goal is achieved, a threshold will have been crossed and sustainable consumption practices will diffuse throughout the affluent industrialised countries.

GAP's Household EcoTeam Program fills the gap between positive attitude and positive action. It provides people with a simple blueprint for how to take practical action to reduce consumption in their daily lives, together with a support and feedback system to help them sustain their good intentions. Over several months, with the help of an EcoTeam (a group of friends, family or neighbours), the Household EcoTeam Workbook, and a coach, participants in the program take concrete actions to create more environmentally sustainable lifestyle practices.

The GAP program spreads by word of mouth and through local community and neighbourhood groups. Over 8,000 households worldwide (representing more than 20,000 people) have participated in the program to date.

GAP is now refining strategies for mobilisation in community-wide participation, neighbourhood by neighbourhood. As a community is mobilised to participate in the program and save resources, this has significant benefits for local landfill, energy, water and transportation issues. The program is now either starting or fully operational in 14 countries.

Marilyn Mehlmann is a change management consultant; co-founder and director of the Swedish Institute for Social Inventions: and the secretary of GAP International. Her current focus is on the social change process.

Marilyn Mehlmann
Stjärnvägen 2
18246 Enebyberg
Sweden

Tel +46 8758 3145
Fax +46 8768 8397

gapinter@ett.se

CIVANO: THE TUCSON SOLAR VILLAGE
Guy Dauncey

The state of Arizona has a steadily growing population, driven primarily by the exodus from California. The City of Tucson has a reputation for environmental responsibility, and working with a wide range of local community organizations, the City has approved the development of a village to be built within the city perimeter on an 820 acre site 30 minutes SE of Tucson city centre, as a demonstration of the marketability of a large scale sustainable community settlement. The village is planned for 5,000 people.

The land is owned by the Arizona State Land Trust, and will be sold by auction to the highest bidder in May 1996, with binding sustainability conditions attached. At the invitation of the City of Tucson, the Trust for Sustainable Development (see below) has been working to refine the current designs, and is a serious contender for purchase and development.

The design for Civano envisages an active village centre with busy commercial, civic and cultural activities and three neighbourhood centres, linked by pedestrian and cycle walkways and narrow tree-lined roads. Half the population will be within a 5 minute walk of the village centre. The sustainability conditions attached to the land through its zoning include a commitment to energy efficiency, using the best available efficiency technologies, including passive solar design. **As solar power generation becomes competitive, Civano expects to lead the country in providing solar-sourced power to the community.**

The sustainability conditions also include water efficiency(water-eficient appliances, xeriscaping, recycling water for irrigation, site specific water harvesting techniques), affordable housing, reduced solid waste, reduced vehicle use, and the generation of one job for every two households.

Written by Guy Dauncey, consultant to the Trust for Sustainable Development.

For more information, write to
John Laswick,
Economic Development Office,
PO Box 27210,
Tucson, AZ 85726-7210
USA

Trust for Sustainable Development,
David Butterfield,
749 Yates St,
Victoria, B.C. V8W 1L6
Canada

workshops

The challenge of Civano is not to build the ideal ecological village but to demonstrate the 'best possible practice' that will sell competitively under market conditions, financed by the private sector. Once this break-through can be achieved, the North American housing market will open itself to embrace ecological village designs. Civano is about the art of the possible, not the art of the perfect.

The Trust for Sustainable Development is a not-for-profit Canadian corporation, based in Victoria, Canada, which works to develop land in a sustainable manner, promoting and implementing the principles of eco-logically and economically sustainable development. Its founder is David Butterfield, who is also President of the South Island Development Cor-poration, the Bamberton developers.

BAMBERTON   Guy Dauncey

Written by Guy Dauncey, sustainability consultant to Bamberton. Guy lives in Victoria, British Columbia, Canada, where he works as an author (writing a major eco-novel about the next millennium) and as a consultant/activist in the field of sustainable community develop-ment.

For further information, write to Scott Andrews, South Island Develop-ment Corporation, 749 Yates St, Victoria, B.C. V8W 1L6, Canada.

Vancouver Island is a magical, beautiful island off Canada's west coast. It has a population of 600,000 people, which grows by 12,000 people every year. There is a strong need for more housing, coupled with strong resist-ance by existing residents to any intensification of the existing urban com-munities.

Bamberton is the site of a huge abandoned cement works, 32km north of Victoria, located on the shores of the Saanich Inlet, an ecologically frag-ile piece of water. The site was bought by four labour union pension funds in 1989 with a view to restoration and development. During 1990, 300 hours of community meetings were held to discover what local feelings were about the site, and what kind of development might be acceptable. The overall response was twofold - "Build it the way things used to be in the old days, emphasizing the traditional values of small-town life", and "Don't trash the environment". Stemming from these mandates, a set of 95 Design Principles was written, laying down the planning framework for an ecologically sustainable new town for 12,000 people, embracing principles of social, economic and ecological wholeness, and a positive vision of the future. **In normal developments, the term 'infrastructure planning' refers to the roads, sewers and services. At Bamberton, in seek-ing to work in a more holistic, integrative manner,** we undertook five levels of infrastructure planning :

A. The Cultural Infrastructure
This sets the vision, and determines the inner values that the planning for the town will embrace. From this, all else follows. (Community participa-tion; 95 Design Principles; the Bamberton Code)

B. The Ecological Infrastructure
There are two main dimensions here, concerning relationship to the past and present (ecological inventory), and relationship to the future (protec-tion, restoration and sustainability). A full ecological inventory showed which areas have specific ecological value, and led to 50% of the land being set aside as parkland, open space and native habitat areas, includ-ing all the ravines and most of the waterfront. Other planning initiatives include the protection of trees; tertiary biological sewage treatment (equiva-lent to solar aquatics in result); the use of natural swales for storm water management; energy and water efficiency measures; environmentally sound building materials; and a comprehensive community recycling and waste reduction strategy.

C. The Community Infrastructure
Urban design based on traditional neighbourhood development princi-ples; narrow streets, small setbacks, back lanes, pedestrian emphasis, three distinct village centres; affordable housing initiatives; cohousing; atten-tion to community-based health care, schools, provision for children, eld-erly; community database for future residents.

D. The Economic Infrastrusture
Comprehensive planning for an effective local economy. Environmental technologies; building; retail; ecotourism; education; telecommuting; the arts; wood products; fibre optic telecommunications; community infor-mation systems; a social and environmental business code; development

of a 300-person Bamberton Business Network; sustainable transportation strategies.

?. The Physical Infrastructure
Roads, sewers, storm drains, utilities, building envelope and site protection, all sensitive to the local ecosystem.

The new zoning bylaws for the proposed town passed 3rd Reading in September 1993, but have subsequently gone into a very detailed and lengthy process of government approval, which may take until 1998 to complete.

THE WISDOM OF THE COMMUNAL ELDERS
Bill Metcalf

The global 'new-age' communal movement is now about 25-30 years old. While most of these new-age communes began as an anarchistic and often hedonistic manifestation of a youth movement, both the participants and the intentional communities which have survived, have aged. Researchers, however, too often address the questions of contribution and survival of new-age communes as if they are still filled with exuberant, long haired, youthful hippies, rather than by seasoned communards with a mean age in the mid forties.

Over the past two years Bill has been conducting biographical research into the life stories and 'wisdom' of communal elders. The elders come from a broad spectrum of intentional communities across Australia. They are the long-term communards who have managed to develop and maintain their communal lifestyle, enthusiasm and critical thinking. Their stories, the stories of communal survival, are both heart wrenching and encouraging.

What can we learn from the stories of these communal elders?

Longevity and cross-generational sustainability are crucial to any meaningful analysis of the contemporary movement. Often the utopian spirit fares much better than the actual communal experiment. An elder from the Dharmananda community in Australia asks, "Are we just a bunch of aging, middle class baby boomers with Buddhist tendencies, trying to maintain a toehold on the 1960's, and will the whole thing just fizzle out after one generation? Or will Dharmananda endure and thus have lasting social relevance?"

Many groups experience a tension between the 'doing' and 'being' aspects of collective life. Striving for radical change tends to take people away from just enjoying each other and sharing everyday life. After all, when one is promoting social revolution it may seem a waste of time to discuss who washes the dishes! Tensions between the 'doing' and 'being' aspects of communal life have no final solution. But when a group devotes more attention to 'doing' through group projects, members come closer, promoting their sense of 'being.'

Communes persist only when people submerge their individuality into the collective reality. That is why most alternative lifestyle groups in Australia are not communes but are alternative (or intentional) communities. Alternative communities attempt to get the best of both worlds, to allow considerable personal autonomy while enjoying the fruits of a more diffuse social collectivity. Intentional communities, however, tend to lose their radical zeal and become 'rural suburbs.'

Although facing innumerable problems, this global new-age communal movement is growing and quite healthy. The diverse stories of these communal elders demonstrate that:
• Communal living attracts and creates fascinating characters.
• A spiritual, beyond-self orientation is almost always needed.
• Leadership is critical, with all forms of community experiencing problems.
• Conflict is endemic and will be resolved — somehow.
• The material, political , spiritual and social planes are entwined.
• Sustainable communal societies are possible but difficult.

Bill Metcalf has lived in and studied communities for over 20 years in Australia and twenty other countries. The results of the first phase of Bill's research have just been published as From Utopian Dreaming to Communal Reality, *by the University of New South Wales Press, Sydney Australia. It centres on ten communities in Australia : Crystal Waters, Tuntable Flals, Chenrezig, Daharmananda, Cennednys, Commonground, Mandala, Moora Moora, The Wolery, and Frog's Hollow.*

The next stage of Bill's research involves 15 communal elders from around the world. The collected life stories and communal wisdom of these participants will be published as The Wisdom of the Communal Elders: Ecospirituality and Social Experimentation *by Findhorn Press in 1996.*

Bill led the workshop with assistance from three communal elders: Albert Bates of The Farm, USA; Mary Ingliss from Findhorn, Scotland; and Glen Ochre from Commonground, Australia.

*Bill Metcalf
50 Mabel St
Highgate Hill
QLD 4101
Australia
metcaf@ens.gu.edu.au
Tel +07 3844 8922
Fax + 07 38448922*

THE GREEN ROOM: THE KIBBUTZ RESPONSE TO THE ECOLOGICAL CRISIS   Jan Bang

Jan Bang is an archeologist, environmentalist, teacher and member of Kubbutz Greer.
Jan teaches seminars on the environment, the peace process and the values of work in the kibbutz. He is a co-founder of the Green Room.

Jan Martin Bang
Kibbutz Gezer
D.N. Shimshon
99786
Israel
Tel   +972 8 9270 464
Fax +972 8 9270 736

The roots of Judaism, both as a religion and as a culture, lie in the natural ecology of the land of Israel. The first task of the kibbutz movement was to develop settlements and the foundation of the modern state of Israel. In environmental terms, this meant tree planting, greening the desert and draining the swamps. At the time, these were seen as progressive environmental actions. Today our criticism of this approach emphasises how sophisticated our ecological thinking has become during the last two generations. The trees could have been mixed species, greening the desert has led to problems with soil salinity and some of the drained areas are now being turned back into swamps and valuable wetlands.

The kibbutz movement can rightly be regarded as one of the major polluters and environmental dangers to Israel. But it cannot be denied that some of the greatest environmental advances have been made by people living on kibbutz. The kibbutz movement is ready to take up the task of caring for the land, with as much enthusiasm as it took over the settling of the land two and three generations ago?

The Green Room opened at the Seminar Centre (Merkaz Hadracha) at Ramat Efal in January 1994. Its purpose is to raise awareness throughout the kibbutz movement on the issues of ecology and the environment. The Green Room was inaugurated with a series of seminars on recycling, environmental planning and architecture, green consumerism, permaculture, organic farming and health. In the following months the Green Room set up plans to promote dialogue and cooperation on environmental issues between Israelis and Palestinians. Development of the West Bank will compound the environmental problems which already challenge the region unless it is carried out with environmental awareness and sensitivity. Air pollution and the contamination of water supplies will face both Israelis and Palestinians in the coming years.

The kibbutz movement is open to co-existence with Palestinians through a peaceful process. The collaboration between the two nations was planned as an open-ended process resulting in education, business and development over three years; culminating with the educational activities being handed over to a self-financing consultancy body. To date, no funding has been found for the proposal and it is on hold. Yet the experience of making new environmental contacts was essential to the Green Room.

In the last year a much clearer picture of the scope and possibilities of the Green Room has begun to emerge.
• A series of day seminars were offered, covering: energy savings through retrofitting existing buildings, health and the environment, permaculture, environmental tourism and water savings in landscaping.
• The kibbutz movement will be represented in meetings with outside bodies engaged in environmental activities.
• The Green Room will maintain links with Palestinian environmentalists.
• A model for an ecological kibbutz will be developed.

In the fast moving world of environmental thinking many streams of ideas meet and cross each other, creating new directions. By fostering working relationships with organisations active in the field of alternative medicine, for example, The Green Room is addressing the issues of food production and organic farming. Awareness of health and nutrition is growing in Israel, as the positive benefits of a cleaner environment are beginning to be appreciated. The history of kibbutz development and the close contact kibbutzim have with immigrants and travellers enables them to offer valuable insight on these issues.

Kibbutzim are an essential part of the eco-village movement. They offer a network of human scale communities based on cooperation and offer an alternative to capitalist development. Environmental awareness and activism are spreading throughout the kibbutz movement. With the help of the Green Room the kibbutz movement will become a social, spiritual *and* ecological model for human settlement.

LOS ANGELES ECO-VILLAGE   Lois Arkin

As Los Angeles continues expanding to accommodate ever larger and more diverse populations, how can we achieve a decent standard of living without sacrificing a better quality of life?

What will be the response of political and grass-roots leadership as it begins to deeply understand the relationships between environmental, social and economic degradation?

As more people in less developed areas world-wide aspire to Los Angeles lifestyles, what responsibility will the city take to model living patterns in balance with the planet's life support systems?

The L.A. Eco-Village seeks to address these complex issues by demonstrating a different way of being in the city. The Eco-Village is a group of neighbours and friends living in a two block, multi-ethnic, working class neighbourhood of about 500, near downtown L.A.. The group believes that a high level of trust and caring enhances the quality of neighbourhood life and provides a social web in which to create larger economic and physical changes such as owning their apartment buildings and removing pavement to provide more open space and regenerate the soil for organic food production. These qualities—caring and trust—also help stabilise neighbourhoods by motivating people to stay.

When the processes of creating an eco-village were begun in 1993, very few residents knew one another, most were fearful of their neighbours, and there were no neighbourhood activities. In the last three years a variety of small, physical projects have been undertaken to help create a sense of interconnectedness amongst neighbours: dozens of fruit trees have been planted, recycling and composting programs have been established, harvests from community gardens provide food for potluck dinners, a pilot apartment recycling project is providing livelihood for young people and saving landfill space, there is a neighbourhood newsletter and news kiosk, and a neighbourhood local exchange trading system (LETS) helps people trade goods and services without cash. In the future the Eco-Village plans to reduce auto dependency by facilitating local employment, organise a small coop farmer's market for selling locally grown organic produce, purchase up to sixteen units of housing for conversion to permanently affordable cooperatives and to install a demonstration grey water reclamation system.

Through working together with their own skills and resources, the L.A. Eco-Village has begun to create changes in their neighbourhood at a pace that can be comfortably incorporated physically, socially and economically. They seek to create a healthy balance between planning and experimentation. People get involved with eco-village processes by working with existing project groups. New project areas are also invited, and there is much opportunity for collaboration, consensus planning and leadership. Developing effective group facilitation and planning processes includes consensus decision making and conflict resolution and becoming a learning neighbourhood in which everyone is both a student and a teacher.

Lois and her colleagues would like to see many other eco-villages grow in their urban area. "Scaling up means sharing what we've learned with other neighbourhoods which want to begin their own paths toward a sustainable future. Doing that kind of sharing closest to home conserves energy and allows for an easier confederation of sustainable neighbourhoods." Lois wants to incorporate Eco-Village into policies at the LA Housing Department and to scale up through a formal relationship with the Coalition of Neighbourhood Developers. The idea will spread, according to Lois, as more and more neighbourhoods realise that their economic and social health is directly related to ecological health. **Eco-Village is really a way of thinking that helps us focus our energies on the quality of our relationships with one another and our life support systems of air, soil and water."**

Lois Arkin has been pursuing a vision she describes as "living lightly on the land" for more than 20 years. She is the founder of Co-operative Resources and Services Project (CRSP), a training and education centre for community barter systems, collaborative housing networks, community loan funds, and other coop endeavours. Lois lives in and coordinates the activities of the L.A. Eco-Village.

Lois Arkin
3551 White House Place
Los Angeles C.A 90004
USA

Tel +1 213 738 1254
Fax +1 213 386 8873

crsp@igc.apc.org

GRASSROOTS CRUSADERS IN THE HEART OF MEXICO
Heidi Bauer

Heidi Bauer is a co-founder and general coordinator of Aztlan Ecological Rescue Centre in the state of Querétaro, Mexico. She is also trained in gestalt therapy, believing that people must first heal themselves before being able to live peacefully with each other and nature.

Heidi Bauer
"Aztlan"
Apdo. Postal 1248
76000 Queretaro Qro.
Mexico

Tel +52 42 12 22 62
Fax +52 42 12 23 81

Romángr250961@
campus.gro.itesm.mx

Mexico is a land of contrasts in many ways. Its mountains and valleys, as well as its beaches and deserts, offer a great biodiversity and variety of beautiful landscapes. Pre-hispanic dwellers had a high respect for nature and lived very much in harmony with it. Today, Mexico suffers from desertification, soil erosion, water scarcity, accelerated population growth, pollution, the disappearance of precious wild life species and many other environmental problems.

In 1983 Enrique and Isabel Sohn and Heidi Bauer moved from Mexico City to the State of Querétaro. They were looking for a ranch where they could start a sustainable community with a healthier outlook, more in harmony with nature. **At that time nobody talked about ecology or environmental consciousness, so very few people understood what these pioneers were trying to do.**

In 1984 the 138 hectare site that was to become the Ecological Rescue Centre was purchased. The site included the ruined remains of a 17th century hacienda which has since been restored. It is a real 'eco' building—with thick adobe and stone walls, and high ceilings that keep the rooms cool even in the most intense heat. This building is meant to become the community centre, library and educational complex.

In 1985 the founders began their efforts to return to Nature what had been lost. The land was studied to determine the best way to use each part of the property. Soil types were studied, native plants and animals were identified and intensive reforestation was began. A well was drilled and a wind-powered pump was installed to provide water for domestic use. Friends of the Ecological Rescue Centre have also helped obtain photovoltaic cells for generating electricity and solar collectors for heating water. Cisterns provide storage for collected rainwater. Gradually, thanks to the reintroduction of biological nutrients, the soil's fertility has increased and its general health is being restored. At Aztlan, the most important features of eco-agriculture include making compost, self-sufficient animal husbandry, organic gardening, water conservation, terraces, reforestation and nurseries. After many years of intensive work and an increasing number of members and volunteers, the Aztlan property is filled with wild meadows, trees and flowers, and the oldest inhabitants of the area, wild animals, have begun to return to the land.

The Aztlan experience is deeply rooted in an environmental lifestyle based on learning-by-doing. The vision of a better quality of life is offered in real life demonstrations and ongoing projects. Aztlan has facilities available for a variety of programs, including permaculture and other specialised workshops with an holistic approach. Aztlan also contributes to the surrounding communities by its participation in the Environmentalists Association of the State of Querétaro, which they co-founded. The most active and serious environmentalists joined forces and are increasingly influencing the inhabitants and authorities towards greater environmental awareness and actions, like proper waste management. Aztlan also works with the Sierra Gorda Group, which is renowned in Queretaro for its important and wide ranging community work, pushing towards more sustainable development, reforestation and conservation of the forests.

Aztlan is an ambitious, collective project. The Centre has formed alliances with national and international environmental and conservationist organisations. Still, as an institution, it needs to be strengthened, mainly economically, in order to be able to continue its development. In the future they foresee the construction of adequate ecological living quarters, as well as areas dedicated to workshops for handicrafts and fine arts, and an area for the processing of produce from the animals and land. There will also be ample grounds for sports and other physical disciplines.

COUNCIL OF ALL BEINGS
Molly Young Brown and Lee Oldershaw

This ritual, created by John Seed and Joanna Macy, offers a conscious experience of both the pain and the power of our interconnectedness with all life. The ritual helps participants to hear the sounds of the earth crying and provides a forum which lets other life forms speak through them.

This Council began by exploring our responses to the crises in the world today through meditation and "Milling"— in which we formed a series of dyads and regarded the other person in the light of the dangers s/he may face in the near future, the commitment this person has to the world, the preciousness of this person's life, and evolutionary and personal history which has brought this person to this moment.

Participants then spent some time alone outside, listening for the call of the Being who wanted to speak through them. They then prepared simple masks from materials available to represent the Beings who had chosen them. The group read together from the book *Thinking Like a Mountain*, a poetic presentation of the names of endangered animals throughout the world.

When all were ready, the group returned to various spots outside and then gathered at a council circle prepared in advance, summoned by a drum beat. Lee and Molly evoked the presence of the Four Directions and Beings from the Past, Present, and Future. Speaking for the Beings who had chosen them, participants told of their experiences, concerns, and feelings in living in a world impacted and devastated by human activities. Various group members took off their masks for a while and sat inside the circle to listen to all this with their human ears. Finally, each Being told what it had to teach humans, or qualities it wanted to share with humans. We ended with everyone once again in human form, full of the grief and the gifts that had been shared. Molly read a poem by Mary Oliver called "Wild Geese" as a kind of benediction.

The group returned indoors to talk about what we had learned, and what intentions we might want to carry away with us. Four people in the group had felt moved to speak for "soil" or "earth" and speculated that perhaps the condition of the soil was of special importance at this time. People spoke of how profound an experience it was to identify so fully with another Being in this way, and to speak from that perspective.The group talked about how the Council can be used in various settings, and Lee shared how she has used the form with children.

In the following days, the group often met up with one another and talked about how the Council continued to affect them and inform their responses to other experiences at the Conference.

Molly Young Brown has worked closely with deep ecologist and Buddhist scholar Joanna Macy for the past four years, pursuing her commitment to systems transformation.

Lee Oldershaw, formerly a Findhorn Foundation educator, currently facilitates personal growth workshops internationally, which integrate psychological and spiritual healing and art.

The poem"Wild Geese" is reprinted as part of Clare Cooper Marcus' plenary presentation.

Molly Young Brown
903 Marylyn Circle
Petaluma CA 94954
USA

Tel +1-707 762 5143
Fax +1-707 762 5143

mollyeco@aol.com

TOWARDS INTEREST AND INFLATION FREE MONEY
Declan and Margrit Kennedy

Daily we are reminded of the world's ecological and economic crises, and of the serious disparities between the rich and poor peoples of the world. What is less apparent is that the present money, land and tax systems create a societal framework that directly contributes to these problems.The solution to our problems must involve a fundamental change in these systems.

The full implication of compound interest is often overlooked. It has been calculated that one penny invested at the birth of Christ at 5% annual interest (the average rate paid through this period of history) would today buy 134 billion balls of gold of the weight of the earth. With interest and compound interest, our money grows exponentially - which sets the stage for pathological growth of our economic system.

Clearly, not all the money in society can go on "earning" 5% interest indefinitely, yet something like this is what we are typically led to expect. In that expectation lies the source of some of our most serious global problems.

Margrit Kennedy is an architect, urban planner and professor of Ecological Design and Construction at the University of Hannover. She is the author of **Interest and Inflation Free Money—Creating an exchange medium that works for everybody and protects the earth** (*Seva International, Okemos, Michigan). Declan Kennedy is an architect and permaculture designer, currently focusing on the relationship between ecology and the built environment.*

Margrit and Declan Kennedy Ginsterweg 4-5 31595 Steyerberg

Tel +49 5764 2158 Fax +49 5764 2368

dkennedy@ lebensgarten.gaia.org

Few people understand how they pay interest and that — in addition to interest on their debts — there is hidden interest in the prices of all the goods and services we buy. This invisible capital charge is less for those items which are labor-intensive, and greatest for those that are capital intensive.Those who have larger amounts of capital to loan receive more than they pay, whereas those who are not so fortunate pay more interest than they receive. Thus the monetary system contains within it a hidden redistribution mechanism which is constantly shifting money from about 80% of the population, who have less, to 10% who have more money than they need. This is true between nations and institutions as well as between individuals. The U.N. World Commission on Environment and Development observes that the roots of the problems on the African continent, for example lie partly in "a global economic system that takes more out of a poor continent than it puts in. Debts that they cannot pay force African nations relying on commodity sales to overuse their fragile soils, thus turning good land to desert." The commission concludes: "Inequality is the planet`s main environmental problem; it is also its main development problem".

There is an inexorable relationship between interest and inflation. Because interest payments on national debt - over time - tend to outrun gross national product, governments tend to close the gap by printing more money which, by the way, is the only way in which inflation can happen. The larger the gap between income and debt, the greater the pressure to reduce the debt by inflation.

The interest system is also associated with the global arms race and the ecological exploitation of the earth. The existence of a huge pool of money for investment creates a constant pressure for large-scale investment - e.g. nuclear power plants, huge dams for hydroelectric power, and arms. In addition to our tendency to take the short-term view, most ecologically sound investments today cannot compete with the money-making power of the money market. Thus capital remains short for most ecologically sound investment (e.g. for utilising solar energy). However, with an interest-free money ecologically sound practices would become"economically" feasible, more easily.

A solution to this systemic problem was proposed in 1890 by a German merchant named Silvio Gesell. The basic idea is to make money a governmental service which is subject to a use fee. In 1932-33, this idea was tested out in a small Austrian town of Woergl when that region of Europe was severely affected by the worldwide economic depression. They issued 32.000 "Free (i.e. interest-free) Schillings", covered by the same amount of ordinary Austrian Schillings in the bank. The town, then, used this currency to pay for public services. The use fee on the use of the money was 1% per month or 12% per year (payable to the town council). This fee had to be paid by the person who held the banknote at the end of the month, in the form of a stamp worth 1% of the note and glued to its back; otherwise the banknote was invalid. This use fee provided incentive for everyone who got paid in Free Schillings to spend these before they used their ordinary money. Some people even paid their taxes in advance in order to avoid paying the use fee. Within one year the Free Schillings circulated an average of over 460 times, over twice the circulation of the ordinary Austrian schillings. The additional goods and services created by this circulation of (460 x 32.000 =) 14.816.000 Schillings contributed a sizable margin of prosperity - at the minimal fee of (12% of 32.000 =) 3.840 Schillings.

In a time when most countries were having severe problems with decreasing numbers of jobs, Woergl reduced its unemployment rate by 25%. When over 300 communities in Austria geared up to adopt this model of local money, the Austrian National Bank saw its monopoly endangered. Its response was to prohibit the town from further printing of its own money. In spite of a long-lasting battle which went up to the Austrian Supreme Court, neither Woergl nor any other community in Europe has been able to repeat the experiment up to the present day.

A more recent proposal by Yoshito Otani substitutes for "alternate money" the mechanism of dual accounts. Each person would have two accounts: a current access account and a savings account. The money in the current account which is at the disposal of the owner continually would be treated like cash and lose as little as 1/2% per month or 6% per year. Those who had more money in their current account than needed for the payment of all expenses in a particular month would be prompted by the use fee to transfer the excess to their savings account, where it would retain its value and from which it would be available for loaning to whoever needed it.

The savings account would not pay interest, and therefore, a person taking out a loan would also pay no interest. But banks would attach risk premium and service charges totalling about 2.5%, as they do now. Thus banks would have an incentive to keep their money working because any of their moneys not loaned out would be subject to the same use fee that everyone else has to pay. **Because people would have an incentive to keep their money in a savings account, where it retains its value, or in some comparable investment, many social and ecological problems would be relieved**. Large private gains through interest would be replaced by small public gains from the use fee. Pressure on overproduction and over-consumption would be reduced - since high capital returns would not be needed to pay interest charges.

It is not immediately apparent why a "fee" on money is preferable to charging interest for loans. The basic reason is that it stops the automatic redistribution of money from the large majority to a small minority and encourages money circulation and investment, whereas interest encourages disparities, speculation and hoarding.

If the above-described monetary reform were to be implemented on a large scale, an accompanying land reform would be required. Without such reform there would be a tendency for surplus money to be attracted to land speculation. Both private and communal ownership of land have their problems. With the capitalist pattern there is a tendency for land ownership to concentrate with powerful individuals and institutions. With the communist pattern there is little incentive to use the land productively. Both Gesell and Otani advocated a combination of private use and communal ownership; a pattern followed by many traditional societies.

Social justice, ecological survival, and human freedom are threatened where societal structures tend to work against these goals. The proposed reforms combine the advantages of capitalism and communism. They promote freedom and enterprise while at the same time promoting social justice and ecological protection. They could reduce the necessity of governmental intervention to a minimum and at the same time create an ecological economy in which goods and services would tend to be produced at an optimum size and level of complexity, because it is there that they would be cheapest and most competitive.

The reforms proposed here will not solve all the world's ills. They could be, however, a critical component of the necessary social and economic transformation of the planet.

CONFLICT RESOLUTION / HOW TO LIVE IN HARMONY WITH ALL CREATION

Hildur Jackson

Hildur Jackson is a lawyer by education and a grassroots activist by nature. She worked for several years in the Nordic Alternative grassroots project for a sustainable Scandinavia. She has twenty years' experience living in one of the first Danish co-housing communities and was instrumental in developing Gaia Trust's eco-village vision.

*Hildur Jackson
Storkevænget 8
2840 Holte
Tel +45 425581
Fax +45 42 55 91
hildur@gaia.org*

Hildur began the workshop by having the group sing "The Leaves are Falling", by the 18th c. Danish author, Grundtvig. In addition to songwriting, Grundtvig also founded the Folk High Schools in Denmark, which were the impetus for the country's community and co-operative movement. He believed that the only education was for life and enlightenment.

Hildur believes that singing is a way of creating resonance. "When a group sings the same tune together, then they're in tune. Singing is a way of creating harmony between people."

Hildur has been involved in the community movement for many years and is in the process of putting together a book on conflict resolution written especially for eco-villagers. The book will contain a series of essays by community elders from around the world. "The world is ready to create eco-villages and to learn to live together. The elements are in place, but a full scale eco-village has yet to be created. Perhaps the biggest obstacle to this is learning to live together. " In the West, we learn that there is only one truth. We need to learn to live with many truths. A group dialogue will create many truths, and we have to learn to live with each of them.

How to Live in Harmony with All Creation will be the title of the book. It is also a positive way of saying conflict resolution. The book will not be focused on personal development or how a group vision is formed, as there are already many books on this subject. It will be about learning to live together, so that we resonate with the land, with nature and with the people around us. Meditation, dancing and ritual are important parts of this resonance, as are more traditional conflict resolution skills, such as dialogue groups and mediation. Really opening oneself to nature is not necessarily verbal.

Conflict is a turning point. It is the opportunity to create something new and wonderful. The vision of eco-villages can be seen as an opportunity to recreate patterns of life that make man whole again.

"But even when the vision is clear, when things are well organised and you are a group of relatively well-functioning beings, you may still have problems in creating an eco-village. You have embarked on a trip to leave a dying culture and create a new one. You need all the strength possible from the divine, from the group and from the land in order to succeed."

The workshop ended with the group sharing their ideas about and experiences with conflict resolution. As a result of the conversation, one member of the group said she now had the courage to return to her community and help solve some of the difficulties they'd been facing.

COMMUNICATION FOR HEALTHY COMMUNITY: COOPERATIVE INQUIRY AND DIALOGUE
Molly and James Brown

New forms of group interaction are evolving today to expand our capacities to think clearly and creatively together. One is "cooperative inquiry," a qualitative research method informed by systems thinking, ecological and diversity concerns, feminism and education, in which participants together decide on the subject and method of inquiry, carry out the chosen actions, and then reflect on their experience and its implications. Another form originated with physicist David Bohm who, with J. R. Krishnamurti, began exploring "Dialogue" in the last years of his life. **Dialogue challenges groups to examine their assumptions more deeply and free themselves of crystalized ideas from the past,** in order to more fully meet the realities of the present. Both cooperative inquiry and Dialogue offer tools for seeking creative solutions to social and ecological problems, and for developing sustainable ways of living. In this workshop, Molly and Jim Brown shared their experiences with both methods, and discussed potential applications of these methods in community building. After initial introductions, participants reflected together in small groups on their own experiences with communication in communities and identified some characteristics of healthy and unhealthy communication. Each group reported its findings to the others.

Under "healthy characteristics," participants mentioned: telling the truth, listening, sharing time, taking risks, staying vulnerable, eye/physical contact, sincerity, sensitivity, explaining context, taking responsibility, making "I" statements, playfulness, spontaneity, "holding a space", commitment to go through the process, distinguishing between disagreement and disapproval, and between responding and reacting.

For "unhealthy" characteristics, they listed: being judgemental, denial of the unpleasant, acting from unconscious assumptions, interrupting, blaming/accusing, abuse of power, seeing the person as the problem, hurrying, being guarded, being superficial, polarizing, acting from fear and insecurity.

This process served as a mini-demonstration of the cooperative inquiry approach, in which participants address an agreed-upon question through cycles of reflection and action. In this case, they imagined that the groups had decided previously to observe communication in their communities (action) and were now meeting to reflect on their findings (reflection). Participants reported finding even this short experience of cooperative inquiry quite valuable.

Jim and Molly then discussed how Dialogue and cooperative inquiry support the characteristics of healthy communication, offering some descriptive phrases for each.

Dialogue:
• a means of uncovering in a group the crystalized patterns of thought and feelings— common to a group or culture— that lead to automatic, non-adaptive responses.
• develops through regular meetings over time.
• no agenda.
• minimum of formal facilitation
• "basic training" for health communication

Cooperative inquiry:
• a method for addressing specific issues/questions in a community that draws on the wisdom and experience of all participants in cycles of reflection and action
• group as a whole defines questions and actions
• short term, task based.
• needs flexibility and willingness to identify and suspend assumptions (as learned through Dialogue)
• light facilitation at beginning.

Molly Young Brown, M.A., M.Div, is author of Growing Whole: Self-realization on an Endangered Planet *and* The Unfolding Self: Psychosynthesis and Counseling. *She teaches psychosynthesis and "Systems Thinking and Social Change" at J.F. Kennedy University in California.*

James Brown, Ph.D. co-created the "Peace in Our Schools" program in Sonoma County, California (along with Molly Brown and Linda Sartor), an innovative progam using "cooperative inquiry" to support teachers in creating a peaceful culture within their classrooms. He and Molly also participate in an on-going "Dialogue" group.

Molly and Jim Brown
903 Marylyn Circle
Petaluma CA 94954
USA

Tel +1-707 762 5143
OwlOnFire@aol.com
mollyco@aol.com

For further reading, the Browns recommend: Thought As A System, *by DavidBohm; and* Human Inquiry in Action, *edited by Peter Reason.*

DEFUSING OUR PERSONAL HIDDEN AGENDAS IN THE PROCESS OF COMMUNITY BUILDING
John Boyd

John Boyd is a teacher, writer, dreamer and eco-visionary who has been inspired by the teachings of E. F. Schumacher, Thomas Berry and Theodore Roszak. John believes that we have no choice but to radically redesign our present way of living and it's material-istic values. He is profoundly committed to rethinking what we mean by quality living and to what really brings us fulfilment.

John Boyd
3 Canterbury Rd.
Islington
Ontario
M9A 5B2
Canada

Tel +1 416 231 0670

Personal agendas are the beliefs, values and opinions that determine how each of us views the world. They are what make one person different from another. When a group of people come together to establish any kind of community, each person brings their own hidden agendas with them. These agendas can be fairly benign, or they can be 'heavy duty' and inflexible. If they aren't disclosed, they can undermine the process of community building.

Personal agendas are not bad in themselves, we all have them. It is only when they are hidden, either from ourselves or from others, that they tend to cause difficulty. The intent of the workshop was to suggest the importance of exercising personal disclosure of these agendas at the very beginning of building a community. By putting their hidden agendas on the table, so to speak, all members have some idea of each others' values, fears, apprehensions, eccentricities concerning belief systems (religious, political, social and ethical), personal background (ethnic, racial, familial), gender preferences and child rearing, etc. The process of disclosure shouldn't be seen as an attempt to foster conformity or uniformity among community members in any way. It is simply a matter of letting each other know what possible elements in our make up might cause friction or conflict of a serious nature further down the road. It should be emphasised that a healthy and vital community must value diversity and differences among its members.

The workshop was designed around small discussion groups of five to eight people. Each group agreed to discuss and disclose some possible personal hidden agendas, as might be the case among members of an intentional community. Each person was given a list of words that could help identify their personal agendas. The list included: desire, greed, love, discipline, unemployment, spirituality, sex, abuse, self-interest, security, trust, truth, art, loneliness, freedom and work.

Many of the words or categories are deeply interrelated. The specific label we give to our personal agendas is often quite arbitrary. The important part is discussion. Most people, given enough time, permission and sense of comfort, can generally get close to their agendas by merely talking (in a conscious and open way) with their small group members. In the workshop the very process of simply talking about these agendas was noted to be most helpful in recognising areas of likely conflict as well as being most useful in defusing their emotional effect.

Having acknowledged the presence of these personal agendas, and only then, can it be decided whether or not they are acceptable to the potential community as a whole, or to one personally, and whether or not there is room for compromise or acceptance within the community of whatever differences have surfaced. Then it can be decided if that person, or myself, might want to withdraw from the community. Ideally there should be no time limit to the process of disclosure. It can be an ongoing experience built into the community's way of life.

How do we reconcile the fact that human diversity is an essential element in any community's ability to be healthy and dynamic, with the effect that some of these personal hidden agendas are potentially detrimental to that healthy and harmony? The importance of hidden personal agendas in the process of community building cannot be underestimated.

THE GLOBAL ECO-VILLAGE NETWORK (GEN) : CREATING REGIONAL NETWORKS

Workshop leaders included: Ross Jackson (Gaia Trust, Denmark), Hamish Stewart (Gaia Villages, Denmark), Albert Bates (The Farm, USA), Max Lindegger (Crystal Waters Permaculture Village, Australia), Declan Kennedy (Lebensgarten Steyerberg, Germany), and Stephan Wik (Gaia Villages, Denmark).

The Global Eco-Village Network began as a small group of representatives from nine eco-village projects working together to promote and develop the eco-village model for sustainable living. The members of GEN's seed group are: Crystal Waters, Australia; Danish Eco-Village Association; Ecoville Projects, Russia; The Farm, USA; The Findhorn Foundation, Scotland; Gaia Villages Denmark (secretariat for GEN); The Gyûrûfû Foundation, Hungary; The Ladakh Project, India; Lebensgarten, Germany; The Manitou Institute, USA. These were chosen for a variety of reasons, including geographical spread, attractiveness as models, ecological and spiritual awareness, and personal contacts. They are not perfect models of sustainable communities, but each has something vital to contribute.

In order to expand the network, the original seed group used the workshops to evaluate interest in creating regional organisations located in Europe, Oceania, and North America. The regionally centred networks encourage active membership by allowing groups to concentrate on issues particular to their geographical area, while providing international contacts. Membership in the Regional Networks is open to any individual, group or network interested in supporting sustainability and the eco-village model. The regional networks are self-organising entities, and will be put in place in other areas, such as South America, Africa, and Asia, as the need arises.

The regional networks can provide:
• Educational opportunities by linking eco-village projects with existing educational systems; creating eco-village exchange programs;
• Aid in developing financing structures for eco-village development and eco-village based businesses;
• A marketing and promotion vehicle for products and services: gathering public support for initiatives, and influencing public opinion, business and government practices;
• Cross-Referencing Services for those seeking: real estate for community, communities to reside in, visit, or intern in; career opportunities/employment needs;
• A pipeline for sharing results of research and seeing the applicability of eco-village models to real world needs and larger structures;
• A philosophical and spiritual forum for discussion and development— such as the exploration of the human relations and processes involved in the migration of people from rural to urban settings,
• A database or library of practical information on alternative technologies; clarification of eco-sustainability and related terms; translation of information in English for non-English speakers; lists and plans for mixed use of new and recyclable materials for home built technologies.

The Internet is a key ingredient in linking the Regional Networks, and a GEN World Wide Web site has now been established on the Net (http: //: www.gaia.org). Members of Regional Networks can create their own Web Pages, and be kept up to date on mailing lists. The Internet is one of the tools that may put villages back on the map as sane, human-scale, self-organising communities. Telecommunications will create many new decentralised work-places in villages, allowing people to remain in close contact with their surroundings, while making contact across the globe.

For more information on GEN, see Ross Jackson's plenary presentation,
The Global Eco-Village Network. *To contact and become part of the Regional Network nearest you, see the Resources section.*

workshops

DIRECTORY OF CONFERENCE PARTICIPANTS

If you're interested in connecting with the movers and shakers in the field of sustainability, a complete directory of the Conference Participants is available through the Findhorn Foundation. The Directory includes participants' addresses, their home country, and their project/community/profession. To receive a copy, please send £5 to

EcoVillage Office,
Findhorn Foundation,
The Park, Forres,
Moray, Scotland IV36 0TZ
Fax +44 (0) 1309 691387
e-mail: ecovillage@findhorn.org

A list of the businesses that participated in the Green Trade Exhibition is also available from the above address upon request.

GLOBAL ECO-VILLAGE NETWORK (GEN) CONTACT ADDRESSES

To become a part of the fastest growing and most exciting network of eco-revolutionaries and pioneers, contact the GEN Regional Secretariat nearest you.

Crystal Waters
Contact person: Max Lindegger
59 Crystal Waters
MS 16, Maleny 4552
Australia
Tel. + 61 74 944 741
Fax + 61 74 944 578
Email: ecosol@peg.apc.org

The Farm
Contact person: Albert Bates
Eco-Village Network
556 Farm Road
Summertown, TN 38483-0090
USA
Tel. + 1 615964 3992
Fax + 1 615 964 2200
Email: albert@gaia.org

Lebensgarten
Contact person: Declan Kennedy
Ginsterweg 4-5
D-31595 Steyerberg
Germany
Tel. + 49 5764 2158
Fax + 49 5764 2368
Email: dkennedy@lebensgarten.gaia.org

The GEN International Secretariat is at Gaia Villages:
Contact person: Hamish Stewart
Skyumvej 101
Snedsted
7752 Denmark
Tel: +45 9793 6655
Fax: +45 9793 6677
E-mail: gen@gaia.org

Visit the Eco-Village Information Service on the World Wide Web:
URL:http://www.gaia.org)

A meeting of the GEN seed group was held from 15-17 October 1995. To receive a copy of the minutes of this meeting contact the International Secretariat.

LETS (Local Exchange Trading Systems)

An excerpt from **"LOCAL EXCHANGE TRADING SCHEMES: GREEN MONEY OR COMMUNITY BUILDING?"**
by Maddy and Tim Harland

LETS is sometimes regarded as only alternative 'green' money, or sophisticated barter. We believe that this approach to LETS is rather limited. LETS does not have to remain in the realm of material exchanges. It can, and in many areas does, evolve into a way of rebuilding links within communities, empowering people ordinarily disempowered by our narrow money system. Rather than just being a trading exchange system, LETS is capable of being a multi-functional "Local Energy Transfer Scheme".

Mono-Money

Money can be multi-functional to those who have it, but in the pursuit of acquiring filthy lucre we can become increasingly mono-functional. These days it is common for people to work weekends and evenings, as well as all week, often keeping the treadmill turning either by an addictive desire for ever increasing amounts of money, or by a more simple need to survive.

Money also acts as a 'barge pole' device because it distances people from each other—the more affluent we become, the more we tend only to associate with rich people as 'social equals' and the more isolated we tend to become. Money also creates secrecy (i.e. Swiss bank accounts); elitism, plutocracy; and the control of land—disempowering those who lack it, socially, psychologically and physically. But it isn't money that is intrinsically bad, it is our fearful tendency to hoard it that empowers *it* rather than ourselves and others.

Liberating LETS

By refreshing and liberating contrast, Local Energy Transfer Schemes enable us to become empowered, freer from fear and multi-functional. No longer are we limited by being 'just ' a computer operator or unemployed person. We can be baby-sitter, seamstress, gardener, organic vegetable grower, artist, coppicer, house painter, poet, mechanic, aromatherapist — you name it, LETS can let us do it, enabling greater versatility and the realisation of otherwise unobtainable ambitions.

LETS isn't secret. A scheme provides information about those that use it — their skills and hobbies, their phone number — and therefore about the resources available in the community. LETS builds bridges, creates links, aids networking and opens the heart of a community by bringing people together rather than isolating them. It enables individuals and communities to implement positive designs: permaculture plots, vegetable box schemes, wholefood co-operatives, building schemes, tree planting, etc.. It also engenders good health by encouraging quality of life and well-being and allows access to low or no cost preventative and natural forms of medicine, organic food, even house swaps and holdiay homes.

In a LETScheme every individual is able to participate, regardless of qualifications, politics or wealth. There are potentially no 'haves' and 'have nots'. Neither does it exclude women, children, men at home with children, the unemployed, the 'un'professionals or the less mobile. Nor are the 'chronologically advantaged' excluded; experience which is so often ignored and devalued in society, can become e a great asset — imagine having LETS apprentice schemes in which older people can pass on skills to younger people!

There is no such thing as an unskilled person. We simply live in a conceptually limited society which educates some of its members to think that they lack skills — and LETS can free us of this limiting misconception. So LETS isn't a one dimensional green money system or a sterling alternative — still deeply limited concepts — LETS *is* empowering, truly democratic and an important tool in the building of sustainable communities.

The following is an excerpt from a brochure put out by the South East Hampshire LETS group (UK), of which Tim and Maddy are founding members.

How It Works

Members trade skills and services on LETS using units of exchange called 'hamlets'. The LETSystem allows members to gain hamlets by offering their skills to anyone in the system and to spend hamlets in exchange for the skills of any other member. Unlike a simple barter system, hamlets can be gained with one member and spent with another.

Using the regularly updated listing, members call up services they require or visit shops or businesses in the system. They write a transaction slip for the agreed value of the goods or services they have used. Each member regularly sends the transaction slips they have received to the LETS coordinator for inclusion in the accounts.

Statements are available by request and a balance of all accounts is open for members to view at all times, and at the quarterly meetings. These meetings are attended by the South East Hampshire LETS Group administrators, known as the officers, and the core group who act in an advisory capacity to them. The meetings are open for all members to attend and participate in decision making. Administrating officers are voted in by the members at an annual meeting.

An Example of LETS Trading

On joining the system I am sent a copy of the membership agreement, a fifty page transaction book and a 'notice board'. This has 10 lines for me to write my offers and requests in—the services or goods I require and those that I offer. These are combined with those of existing members to form a directory of offers and requests that is subdivided into categories. This is also included in the membership package as are the regular updates to it.

Sitting there looking through my directory, I realise that I have a brochure to produce. It needs some artwork and I am hopeless at artwork. At the moment I cannot find a designer. But wait a minute, Emma is offering graphic design on the LETSystem. I get on the phone to her and we agree that she will do the work for 50 hamlets. Oh, and she wants a fiver to cover her sterling costs, stationery and such. We have a deal.

Later that week I get my artwork, write a transaction slip to Emma for 50 hamlets and raid my piggy bank for five one pound coins to cover her sterling costs. Emma sends my transaction slip to the LETS office.

The administrator clears the 50 hamlets to leave my account and go into Emma's. She now has 50 hamlets in her account and she is thinking about asking John to reupholster her sofa.

As for me, I do not owe Emma anything. I have just made a commitment to supply 50 hamlets of work to the members in the scheme, all of them and any of them. There are plenty of ways to do this. Tim wants some help with painting and decorating; Liz needs some computer training; or, I could cut up some logs and offer those.

This is not barter. With a barter system, I would have to repair Emma's sofa (a grim prospect for both of us), or the alternative is no trade. With LETS, not only can we all trade but we can do so on our own terms.

The Benefits

Hamlets can only be used to trade locally with members of the South East Hampshire LETS Group. This encourages people to use local shops and services, increases local trade, stimulates the local economy and helps the community to thrive and prosper.

One great advantage of LETS is that you can start spending before you start earning. Indeed, it is essential that some people do this, because the system has no cash, so the very first transaction can only be paid for by someone going into 'commitment'. This expression is used instead of debt, because there is no stigma attached to having a minus balance in LETS (nor any interest charged). In fact, the total of all minus balances inevitably must equal that of the plus balances at anyone time. The commitment is to the local community and without commitment, the system cannot work.

SUGGESTED READING

Journals

COHOUSING, CONTEMPORARY APPROACHES TO HOUSING OUR-SELVES, The Journal of the CoHousing Network.

Started in 1993, this quickly growing network seeks to promote and support CoHousing in North America by providing news and information about the development process, management issues and life in CoHousing communities. Published by the Cohousing Network, P.O.Box 2584, Berkeley, CA 94702, USA.   Tel +1 510 526 6124

COMMUNITIES, THE JOURNAL OF COOPERATIVE LIVING

Published quarterly by the Fellowship for Intentional Communities. Provides good coverage of issues, ideas and information about intentional communities and cooperative living. The Summer 1996 issue will be devoted to the subject of eco-villages. Contact: The Fellowship of Intentional Communities, Rt 1, Box 155-C, Rutledge MO 63563, USA. Tel +1 816 883 5545

EARTHWORD, THE JOURNAL OF SOCIAL AND ENVIRONMENTAL RESONSIBILITY

This well-produced journal provides problem-solving information on topically focussed issues such as Sustainable Urban Landscape, Wise Water Management, Transportation Planning, Alternative and Indigenous Architecture, The Sacredness of the Land. Excellent Resource Lists. Contact: Lynne Elizabeth, 639 Pearl Street, Laguna Beach, Ca 92561, USA. Tel +1 714 494 8591, Fax +1 714-494-2824, e-mail lynne@deltanet.com

ECO-DESIGN, JOURNAL OF THE ECOLOGICAL DESIGN ASSOCIATION,

New UK publication with good articles on all relevant aspects of ecological building and design. 20 High Street, Stroud, Gloucestershire, GL5 1AS, England.

EUROTOPIA, LEBEN IM GEMIENSCHAFT

A quarterly newsletter focusing on German communities. Occassional updates on European contacts and projects. Published by Eurotopia, Hasenhof 8, 71540 Murrhardt, Germany. Fax +49 (0) 7192 3218 Price DM 48 per annum.

The IN CONTEXT Sustainability Series

Twice winner of the Utne Reader's Alternative Press Award for best coverage of immerging issues, has been inspiring and educating people in the " how to move towards a more sustainable future" for over 12 years. To order, contact Creatura Books, P.O. Box 718 Pt. Reyes Station, CA 94956; Tel +1 800 306 1778, Fax +1 415 663 8440 e-mail: CreaBooks@aol.com   (Visa/Master Card accepted.) See the Selected WWW Sites for *Context Institute* and *In Context* on line.

ONE EARTH,

Quaterly magazine of the Findhorn Foundation Community. Lots of good articles on a real aspiring eco-village. Tells it like it is warts and all. One Earth Ltd, The Park, Findhorn, Forres IV36 0TZ , Scotland Tel +44 (0)1309 691128, Fax +44 (0)1309 691639

PERMACULTURE MAGAZINE — ECOLOGICAL SOLUTIONS FOR EVERYDAY LIVING

A fantastic source for ideas and networking links in permaculture, LETS. For a FREE copy, contact: Permanent Publications, Hyden House Limited, Little Hyden Lane, Clanfield, Hampshire PO8 0RU, England. Tel +44 (0)1705 596500, Fax +44 (0)1705 595834. e-mail: permaculture@gn.apc.org

Sources

The Findhorn Conference Ecological Book Fair, coordinated by the Phoenix Community Store and Christiane Fischer was a raging success during the conference. Space won't permit for all of the book titles to be listed here, but if you're interesed in a complete list please contact the Phoenix Community Store. Many of the conference participants—plenary speakers workshop leaders and others—have titles listed.

>Phoenix Community Store
>The Park
>Findhorn
>Moray IV36 OTZ
>Scotland
>Tel +44 (0)1309 690110
>Fax +44 (0)1309 690933

Creatura Books can provide any book in print and specializes in books or sustainability, deep ecology, systems thinking, ecopsychology, social justice, etc. They donate 5 - 10% of every order to one of a list of transformative non-profits, according to the customer's choice.

>Creatura Books
>903 Marylyn Circle
>Petaluma
>CA 94954
>USA
>Tel/Fax +1 707 762 5143
>e-mail mollyeco@aol.com

Permanent Publications are a small, independent publisher and book distributer specialising in books and videos on permaculture, alternative technology, organic gardening,revitalising community and other related subjects. They also practise permaculture at their 3rd acre site and are involved in local sustainable projects

>Permanent Publications
>Hyden House Limited
>Little Hyden Lane
>Clanfield
>Hampshire PO8 0RU
>England
>Tel +44 (0)1705 596500
>Fax +44 (0)1705 595834.
>e-mail: permaculture@gn.apc.org

Titles

Many plenary speakers and workshop leaders are authors, as well as activists and innovators. In most cases, their book titles are listed as part of the plenary and workshop sessions. To order a title listed in these Proceedings, or get a complete listing of the books written by plenary and workshop leaders, contact one of the *Sources* above.

Hall, Keith and Peter Warm. *Greener Building: Products and Services Directory*. Association of Environment Conscious Building, 1992. A directory with good background information on natural resources, energy and industrial processes as well as products and suppliers of ecological materials.

Henderson, Hazel. *Building a Win-Win World*. Berrett-Koehler, San Fransisco. 1996. Hazel is a self-taught alternative economist who puts the mainstream economists to shame with her vision, her values, and her people-centred common sense. This is her latest book, due out sometime in 1996.

Hawken, Paul. *The Ecology of Commerce : A Declaration of Sustainability*. Harper Business, NY, 1993. Paul is a businessman who has thought longer, harder and deeper than just about anyone else in the business world about just how do we reconcile the process of business with the needs of planetary sustainability. He also wrote *The Magic of Findhorn* almost 30 years ago!

Pearson, David. *Earth to Spirit, In Search of Natural Architecture*. Gaia Books, 1994. Essential for anyone interested in beautiful, natural built forms. Great images and photos.

Peck, M. Scott. *The Different Drum*. Arrow, 1990. How to rebuild communitites, work together as individuals and groups with tolerance and love to transform our world into a true community.

Whitefield, Patrick. *How to Make a Forest Garden*. Permanent Publications, 1996. A detailed practical guide to temperate forest gardening, using the principles of natural woodlands/forests for creating a highly productive and sustainable garden. Design principles, plants descriptions and practical tips for planting your own site.

SELECTED WORLD WIDE WEB (WWW) SITES

Context Institute and *In Context* :
     http://www.context.org
Developing Ideas:
     http://iisd1.iisd.ca/didigest/
Earthword:
     http://www.earthword.com/
Energy Efficiency and Renewable Resources:
     http://solstice.crest.org/social/eerg/index.html
Findhorn Press:
     http://www.gaia.org/findhornpress/
Framework Convention on Climate Change:
     http://www.iisd.ca/linkages/climate/climate.html
GreenClips :
     http://solstice.crest.org/sustainable/greenclips/info.html
Global Ideas Bank :
     http://www.newciv.org/worldtrans/BOV/BOVTOP.HTML
New Civilization Network :
     http://www.newciv.org/worldtrans/newcivnet.html
International Society for Ecological Economics
     http://kabir.umd.edu/ISEE/ISEEhome.html
Office of Research Services:
     http://solar.rtd.utk.edu/default.html
Permaculture FAQ :
     http://csf.colorado.edu/perma/faq.html
Permanent Publications:
     http://www.uea.ac.uk./~e415/home.html.
Pete's Pond Page:
     http://reality.sgi.com/employees/peteo/index.html
PlanetKeepers:
     http://galaxy.tradewave.com/editors/wayne-pendley/plankeep.html
Sustainable Communities Network:
     http://www.cfn.cs.dal.ca//Environment/SCN/SCN_home.html
Sustainable Earth Electronic Library:
     http://envirolink.org/pubs/index.html
World Scientists' Warning to Humanity:
     http://newciv.org/worldtrans/whole/warning.html

USEFUL GROUPS AND ORGANISATIONS

Canadian Healthy Communities Network, 541 Sussex Drive, 2nd flr, Ottawa ON, K1N 6Z6, Canada. Tel +1 613 562 4646,   Fax +1 613 562 4648

Ecological Design Association, The British School, Slad Rd, Stroud, Glos GL5 1QW, UK. Tel +44 (0)1453 765575, Fax +44 (0)1453 759211 (David Pearson, Herbert Girardet, Victor Papanek)

EcoVillage Training Centre, Albert Bates, The Farm, PO Box 90, Summerton, TN 38483, USA. Tel +1 615 964 3992, Fax +1 615 964 2200

EcoDesign Centre, #208, 2130 West 3rd Ave, Vancouver, BC V6K 1L1, Canada.
Tel +1 604 738 9334, e-mail ecodesign@freenet.vancouver.bc.ca (Shelley Penner)

Gaia Trust, Skyumvej 101, 7752 Snedsted, Denmark.
+45 97 93 66 55, Fax +45 97 93 66 77 (Ross Jackson)

International EcoVillage Design Society, PO Box 11645, Berkeley, CA 94712, USA. Tel +1 510 869 5015,   Fax +1 415 332 5808, e-mail ecodesign@igc.apc.org (Sim Van de Ryn and friends)

International Centre for Sustainable Cities, #1150-555 West Hastings St, Harbour Centre, PO Box 12071, Vancouver, British Columbia, V6B 4N5, Canada. Tel +1 604 666 0061, Fax +1 604 666 0009 (Director: Alan Artibise)

International Sustainable Development Network, Daybreak International, 3914 N.Marshfield, Chicago, IL 60613, USA. Tel +1 312 880 1391, Fax +1 312 880 1367
(Nancy Skinner, Rob Gilman, Pliny Fisk, Robert Berkebile)

LØS (Landsforeningen for Økosamfund) , Skyumvej 101, 7752 Snedsted, Denmark. +45 97936655, Fax +45 97936677.

Third International EcoCity Conference, Yoff, Senegal, January 8-12th 1996 Annabel Taylor-Hall, Cornell University, Ithaca, NY 14853, USA.
Tel +1 607 255 8276, Fax +1 607 255 9985, e-mail ecovillage@cornell.edu

UN Conference on Human Settlements (Habitat II), Istanbul, 1996

UNDP-LIFE (Local Initiative Facility for Urban Environment)

Urban Ecology Center, 405 14th St, #701, Oakland, CA 94612, USA. Tel +1 510 549 1724, e-mail urbanecology@igc.apc.org

Many thanks to Guy Dauncey, who contributed several book titles, WWW sites, and Groups and Organisations. He is so well-informed and helpful, Guy deserves to be listed as a resource in and of himself. He can be contacted at:
    2069 Kings Rd, Victoria, BC, Canada V8R 2P6
    Tel/Fax +1 604 592 4473
    gdauncey@islandnet.com
Finally, all my gratitude goes to the Gaia Trust for employing me to put this book together!

—Jillian Conrad (Editor)

resources

Findhorn Press presents

SIMPLY BUILD GREEN

A Technical Guide to the Ecological Houses at the Findhorn Foundation
by John Talbott
Preface by Jonathon Porritt

Simply Build Green is a detailed description of the theory, practice and products used in the Eco-Village Project at Findhorn. It is a combination of standard building techniques and methods, such as foundations and framing — necessary to good quality housing — and the basic philosophy of ecological building and its application.

This book is in answer to hundreds of requests for information about our buildings and ecological work. It is an invaluable resource for professionals in the building trade, including architects, engineers and builders as well as individuals of all levels of experience including DIY enthusiasts who want to convert their loft in an environmentally friendly way.

Pbk   *224 pages*   *£9.95/US$17.95*   *ISBN 1 899171 90 8*

IN PERFECT TIMING

Memoirs of a Man for the New Millennium
by Peter Caddy

In another age legends would have sprung up about the life of Peter Caddy, co-founder of the famous Community at Findhorn and a respected leader in the New Age movement. Early in his life, Peter surrendered himself to the will of God and from this gained an unshakable faith that served him and others throughout his life.

He also gave himself completely and unconditionally to life, embracing it with zest, courage and delight. There was nothing otherworldly about Peter. He was a man of action who thoroughly enjoyed taking on a challenge — the greater the better. Whether serving in the wartime RAF, climbing the Himalayas in Tibet, managing a luxury hotel on spiritual principles or running a New Age community, he climbed every mountain God put in front of him. He married five times and fathered six children. As a consequence, his life reads like an adventure novel: it is a ripping good yarn, which is all the more powerful because it is true.

He was not a philosopher, nor was he particularly self-reflective. He was a visionary and he believed in people, always drawing out the best in them. Everything he did was on a giant scale. Peter Caddy was killed in a car accident shortly before his 77th birthday: even his death was dramatic... In this book, Peter, a master storyteller, takes us on a journey of inspiration, action and spirit. We also participate in his struggles, hardships and initiations, but with Peter, problems and challenges are met head-on with indomitable positive thought and action.

His legacy to us all is the knowledge that following our inner guidance — God's will — is not only an exciting, wonderful adventure, it can also change the world.

Hbk   464 pages + 16 pages of illustrations   *£19.95/US$28   ISBN 1 899171 26 6*